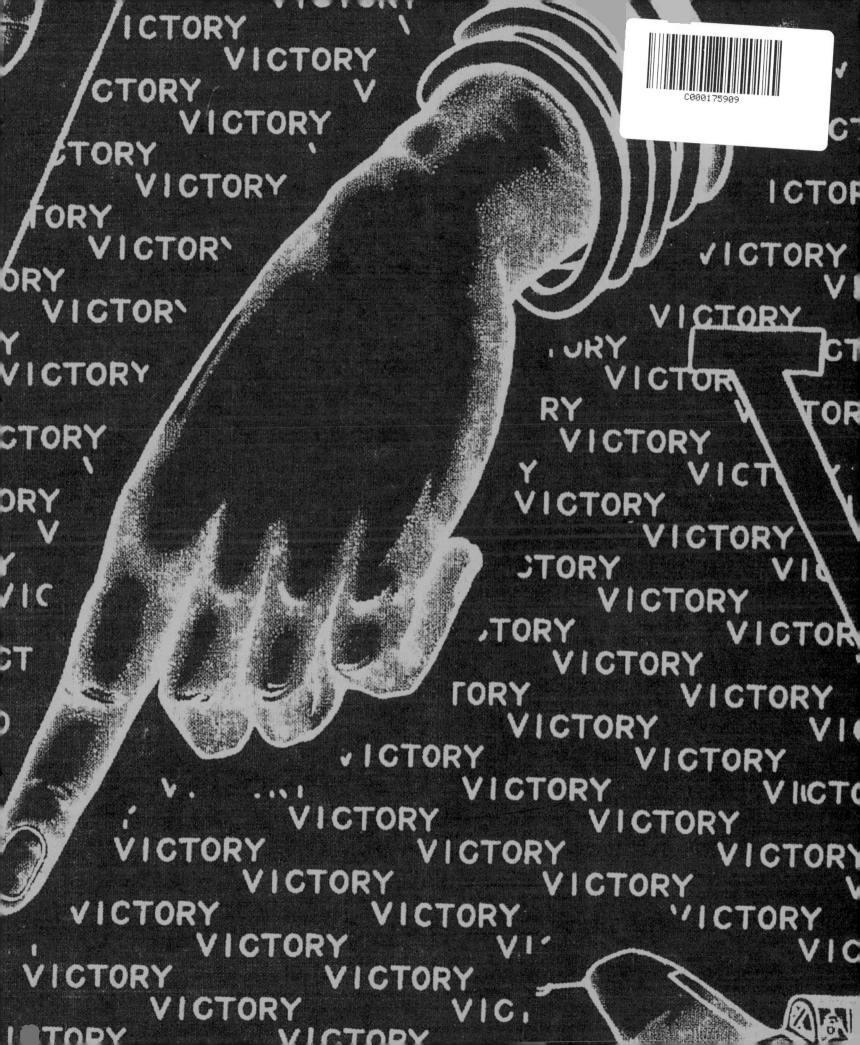

NIGEL CAWTHORNE

THE NEW LOOK

THE DIOR REVOLUTION

NIGEL CAWTHORNE

THE NEW LOOK

THE DIOR REVOLUTION

Special thanks to British Vogue
for their time, effort and contribution from their unique Archive

Editor: Mike Evans
Assistant Editor: Humaira Husain
Production: Melanie Frantz
Picture Research: Wendy Gay
Art Director: Keith Martin
Design: Birgit Eggers

First published in in 1996 by
Hamlyn an imprint of
Reed Consumer Books Limited
Michelin House, 81 Fulham Road,
London SW3 6RB
and Auckland, Melbourne,
Singapore and Toronto

Produced by Mandarin Offset
Printed and bound in Hong Kong

It's a dream... it's HARELLA

FASHION GO

'ANY POWER WHATSOEVER IS DESTINED TO FAIL BEFORE FASHION. IF FASHION SAYS SKIRTS

DES TO WAR

'...RE SHORT, YOU WILL NOT SUCCEED IN LENGTHENING THEM, EVEN WITH THE GUILLOTINE.'

Mussolini

The 1940s were a period of extraordinary upheaval and, in the struggle between totalitarianism and the free peoples, fashion was on the front line. Even the dictators responsible for starting World War II acknowledged that. In the 1930s, Mussolini warned Hitler: 'Any power whatsoever is destined to fail before fashion. If fashion says skirts are short, you will not succeed in lengthening them, even with the guillotine.'

Despite the terrible slaughter that engulfed Europe, America and the Far East, men and women still concerned themselves about how they looked. For many, it was vital to maintain some elegance and human dignity among the horrors of war. Even governments recognised that decent clothing was an essential element in building morale. Clothes manufacture was an essential part of the war effort. Despite shortages and restrictions, governments went out of their way to provide their people with the best possible clothing.

The German Occupation of Paris on 14 June 1940 put the centre of world fashion behind enemy lines as far as the British, and later the Americans, were concerned.

By now, Chanel had already closed down her house. Three leading couturiers – the Englishman Captain Edward Molyneux (in fact, he was Irish with Hungarian blood, but was always considered English), Elsa Schiaparelli and Lucien Lelong – shut up shop and headed south ahead of the invading Germans. Molyneux suggested that they divide his branch in Biarritz into three and work from there. But when France capitulated on 22 June, it was no longer safe for a British passport holder to stay in the country. Molyneux and Charles Creed escaped on the last ship leaving from Bordeaux.

Schiaparelli had a contract to lecture in the US and headed for New York. But as official head of the Chambre Syndicale de la Couture Parisienne,

(above right)

The Great Dictators:

Benito Mussolini and

Adolph Hitler exchanging

fashion notes in 1940

(below)

Coco Chanel (right) in

1931, with the French

actress Ina Claire

Lelong decided that he had no choice and must go back to Paris and deal with the devil directly.

Back in Paris, Lelong found the fashion industry in chaos. Having been cut off from lucrative exports, some fashion houses had already gone out of business. The Germans had broken into the offices of the Chambre Syndicale and seized all the records relating to couture exports. Eager to get their hands on that money, the German High Command ordered the CSCP to close down. The couturiers were to make their way to Germany. The plan was to move what was left of Parisian couture lock, stock and barrel to Berlin and Vienna.

Lelong, however, was determined to thwart this plan. He argued that the French fashion industry depended, not just on the star couturiers, but the manufacturers and suppliers as well. In Paris, there was based a network of subcontractors who made hats, gloves, handbags, jewellery, buckles, belts and buttons. There were also embroiderers, weavers, make-up artists, hairdressers and representatives of the textile companies. Any sort of attempt to move the industry would destroy this infrastructure and with it the expertise that had been built up since the sixteenth century.

Couturier Lucien Lelong, the saviour of more than ninety Paris fashion houses during the years of the German occupation

France's supremacy in silk and lace making was beyond doubt and Lelong maintained that it would be a mistake to take the designers from the milieu of elegance where they found their inspiration. As America had not yet come into the war, the Germans needed dollars that the Parisian industry brought in. The German High Command saw sense and the order was rescinded.

Instead, the Germans decided to appoint their own fashion director to run the industry – Maggy Rouff's husband, Besançon de Wagner. But Lelong continued as his deputy, dealing with the artistic aspect of the industry.

Single-handedly, Lelong is credited with saving 112,000 skilled workers from compulsory labour in German factories and, in all, 92 leading fashions houses stayed open though only twelve where extended privileges.

Textile shortages meant that the collections were smaller. Pre-war, three thousand dresses were shown a year. During the Occupation, that dropped to about a hundred.

Some natural fibres like wool and silk soon became extremely rare. The French population had to make do with artificial materials, which were rationed under a points system, but Lelong did manage to get a special allowance for the couture trade, based on pre-war and not current business.

Some items, such as ribbons, were not rationed, so the couturiers used a lot of them. Rags, wood shavings, newspapers and other unusual materials were also used.

Lelong also obtained permission for couture creations to escape clothes rationing. The idea of unrationed clothes during the war attracted a broader range of clients to *haute couture* than ever before. The middle classes began visiting the salons. And there were also wives and girlfriends of German officers and wartime profiteers. Christian Dior once remarked that many of *haute couture*'s new wartime clients would be shot when the war was over.

The Allied nations took a very dim view of the couture's pact with the Germans. They viewed it a collaboration. But Lelong and the other couturiers who remained open were farsighted. If they had simply refused to trade with the enemy, the whole structure of the industry would have collapsed. Skills built up over generations would have been lost and when Liberation finally came, there would be nothing left.

Throughout the Occupation, the couture houses played a cat and mouse game with the German authorities. They lived in fear of their staff being taken off into labour camps. At the same time, they cheated the Germans as much as possible. They also helped each other out when they fell foul of the authorities. When Madame Grès and Balenciaga were closed for a few weeks by the Germans for exceeding their textiles rations, the other houses finished off their collections for them.

Madame Grès also took a principled stand and refused to sell to the wives and mistresses of German officers. She came up with collections which featured the red, white and blue of the French flag and was threatened with closure. When Nazi propaganda minister Joseph Goebbels heard that Madame Grès was refusing to sell her clothes to Germans, he turned up on her doorstep with a squad of storm troopers. But Grès's sales assistant turned them away, explaining that Madame was busy designing her new collection. In fact, she was sewing together yards of Lyon silk to make a huge tricolour. When she hoisted it out of her window, she was finally closed down.

Even the couture houses who did serve Germans did their bit for the war effort. While British and American designers were cutting back on the use of fabric, French couturiers were extravagant, as they figured the resources they were wasting were not theirs, but the Germans.

The editor of the French *Vogue* Michel de Brunhoff found he could not continue to publish the magazine without some compromise and even collaboration, and closed it for the duration of the war, while the British and American editions of the magazine continued. This was a tacit admission that Paris had relinquished its role as the centre of the fashion world.

Below, a hat by the famed milliner Lilly Daché with floral decoration in 'non-priority' wood Insert, a 1939 dress by Mainbocher, soon to return from Paris to his native America

A dress by Chanel as it appeared in a 1939 edition of the UK *Vogue*, with a very definite French tri-colour inspiration

British-based Captain Edward Molyneaux, whose fashion house had opened in Paris in 1919 with branches active in Monte Carlo, Cannes, Biarritz and London by the mid-thirties

Free from the influence of the Parisian fashion houses, designers in England and America felt to go their own way. Molyneux and Angèle Delanghe set up business in London. The American couturier Mainbocher left Paris for New York. And Schiaparelli spent the war in the US. She opened a boutique in New York, though her couture house continued in her absence. Yet these couturiers did not wield the influence they had had when they were all together in Paris.

America's ready-to-wear industry was much more highly developed than that in the UK. But it had followed Paris more slavishly than Britain. With the start of the war in Europe, there was an explosion of creativity among young designers. They scoured the US for uniquely American styles. Designs produced during this crucial period had a huge influence on casual clothes since the war. Both the T-shirt and the universal appeal of blue denim jeans originated in the war.

World War II forced Britain to develop a huge ready-to-wear industry. Molyneux and some of the top couturiers of the day were co-opted into the Utility scheme, producing clothes for rich and poor. Never before had a mass of British people been so well dressed, giving them a taste for quality clothes lasting long after the war. However, war meant shortages, and styles were necessarily conservative and drab. When the war was over, the world was ready for something new. It got it in 1947, in Christian Dior's first collection as a couturier.

Dubbed the New Look, it aped the opulence of *la belle epoque,* the time immediately before World War I when the century was young and optimistic. Dior's New Look seized the world's imagination. It exploded like no style before or since. The other couturiers had no choice but to follow Dior's lead. The New Look took over the entire ready-to-wear industry. Its influence was seen in art, architecture and other areas of design. And although Dior turned his back on the New Look in 1954, it can still be seen as the foundation of post-war fashion.

From *Femina* magazine in 1948, a portrait of Elsa Schiaparelli, who had moved to New York during the War, by the illustrator Etienne Drian

STYLE AND

SOCIETY

Copyright
1909
Theo. C. Marceau
Ny.

A glamorous society lady photographed in 1909, typical of the *belle epoque* style of the Edwardian period just before World War I

Previous page: the bright young things of the 'Flapper' generation of the Twenties contrasted sharply with the soup kitchens endured by millions during the Depression

The world, of course, had been through a war before and the changes fashion of the 1940s in some ways were an echo of what happened in World War I and its aftermath.

When Europe went to war in 1914, little changed at first. Women continued to wear the extravagant Edwardian styles of *la belle époque*. Their role, it was thought, was to remain elegant and gracious, to soothe and inspire the weary warrior when he returned home. But by 1915, it was clear that the war was not going to be over quickly and that women were going to be called on to take a more active role. The hobble skirt quickly disappeared to be replaced by a shorter, fuller skirt that gave a greater freedom of movement.

Women slowly started to move into the offices and factories. Even women who were not moving into paid employment began to do voluntary work to aid the war effort. As maids found that factory work paid better, many middle class women found that, for the first time, they had to look after their own home and family.

As women replaced men in factories, pamphlets warned them against wearing tight corsets and stiff skirts in the workplace. Although it was considered daring at first, women began to wear trousers for heavy work. Overalls were also found to be practical rather than decorative. Munitions workers wore boilers suits and land girls breeches. World War I saw women in trousers for the first time.

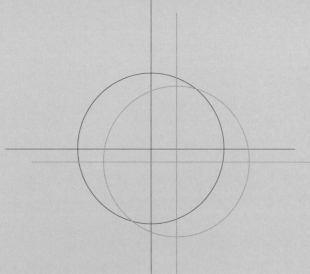

Although this was kept strictly to the workplace to begin with, many women enjoyed the freedom trousers offered and, in the post-war decades, trousers became a fashion item.

Women were also encouraged to wear caps. Some gave up the struggle to keep their hair clean and lice-free in harsh war-time conditions and had it cut short. Again this was a fashion that would have post-war consequences.

As the war dragged on, large numbers of women found themselves in uniform – there were nurses, policewomen, drivers and conductors on the buses, trains and railways. The uniforms deliberately tried to play down women's femininity. However, these uniforms usually had fairly short skirts as working women needed to be able to move around relatively unhindered.

As more women were bringing home a wage packet, the fashion market grew. Women working in dangerous workshops could bring home as much as £5 a week, with overtime. Middle-class society was shocked that factory workers were buying fur coats for themselves. But the fashion industry did not care where all the new money was coming from. The pretty, feminine styles packed shop windows. These had a new simplicity to cater for women who were used to the freedom of overalls and trousers at work. Many of these wartime styles also emulated uniforms, so civilians could be seen supporting the war in their fashion.

The First World War saw women taking on men's roles, often for the first time, like this London bus conductress posing for the camera in 1917

20's

A thoroughly Modern miss from the late Twenties,
complete with the obligatory cigarette holder and trousers
inspired by men's Oxford bags fashionable at the time

After World War I, there was a return to more formally feminine, pre-war fashions. Hemlines were back down nearly to the ground in 1923. But they were up to the knees in 1925. Despite many fluctuations in hemlines since, they have never descended all the way to the floor again.

The 1920s were the age of the flapper. After the slaughter of almost an entire generation of young men in World War I, there was a gross imbalance in the sexes. Women became boyish. They rode on motorbikes, flew planes and challenged men in almost every field. Bosoms and hips were definitely out. The perfect figure was thought to be slim and straight up and down.

The new clean lines of the figure was youthful. It also reflected the ideas in other fields of design – particularly architecture and furniture design – that were being developed at the time. Everything had to be absolutely Modern.

Stays and corsets were abandoned. Brassieres were worn, but only to flatten the breasts rather than accentuate them. Bulky petticoats were dropped in favour of slips and underwear was reduced in weight by the use of rayon. All of the fabrics used in the 1920s – silks, crêpe de chine, rayon and jersey – were light. A woman in the 1920s wore clothes that weighed around one-tenth of those of her Victorian counterpart. And they bought their clothes off the peg.

The shortage of young men meant that more women went into employment. And working women tended to dress like men with their suits made along men's lines. Career women would have 'tailor-mades' made up by men's tailors. Women would also wear plus-fours, men's dinner jackets and lounging pyjamas for evening and beachwear.

Women cut their hair short, in a bob, single or Eton crop. Meanwhile, men grew their hair longer until men and women's styles were almost identical.

Woman also smoked in public and wore make-up. This had been considered immoral in Victorian times but, in the 1920s, the dark Cupid's bow lips, plucked and penciled eyebrows and the ashen powdered faces were borrowed directly from the movie screen.

In 1929, the Men's Dress Reform Party was formed. It aimed to sweep away the old, formal styles of dressing which were very restrictive and also uncomfortable. Many of its ideas seemed wild and eccentric, but men's clothing in the 1920s became much more casual. Baggy plus-fours and huge Oxford bags emulated skirts. Knitwear in bright colours became fashionable with both sexes and the popularity of golf brought with it the Argyll and other diamond patterns in sweaters, cardigans and socks.

Despite the convergence of the sexes, in evening wear particularly, never had more female flesh been so exposed. Legs, arms, chest and back, were all revealed by the wearers of the slinky sheath dresses held up by shoe-string straps that were all the rage in the late 1920s. Beige stockings gave the illusion of bare legs. Fine rayon was used instead of thick wool or cotton – and it was much cheaper than silk.

Outdoor menswear in the Twenties was strong on plus-fours, patterned Argyll sweaters and matching socks

Viewed from the 1990s, the 1930s are mainly remembered for the Great Depression, bringing mass unemployment, soup queues, hunger marches and the rise of totalitarianism in Europe. Yet, for those who could still afford it, the 1930s were the most stylish and glamorous decade of the century.

Following the Wall Street Crash of 1929, millions of people had been pitched into a financial abyss. However, many retained their wealth, but it would have been seen as tasteless to draw attention to it. Society photographer Cecil Beaton remarked in 1930: 'Even if you haven't lost money, you have to pretend you have.' So after all of the vulgar ostentation of the 1920s, everything became more elegant and restrained.

The 1930s were the era of Fred Astaire and Ginger Rogers, who became icons of effortless elegance. They first appeared in *Flying Down to Rio* in 1933 and, for the rest of the decade, made a picture a year. But while Fred was donning his white tie and tails, there was a wilder kind of dancing that came from black people in America. Two of the most widespread were the Lindy-Hop and the Big Apple – a forerunner of the Jitterbug. This was unrestrained and acrobatic, and required different garb altogether. Men now wore loose trousers and tight sweaters, while women wore sweaters or blouses and short-flared or pleated skirts, usually with white bobby sox and flat shoes.

After the schoolboy figures of the 1920s, in the 1930s, women rediscovered their bosoms and waists returned to their natural place. Hemlines dropped with the economic slump. Those who could not afford to buy new dresses added bands of contrasting material or fur to the hem of the dress. And they added similar bands to the collar and cuffs to make it look like the garment had been designed that way.

Coco Chanel showed an instinctive feeling for the times by showing a collection of evening dresses made in cotton – a practical, economic, washable fabric. This also allowed her to slash 50 per cent off her prices in 1932. New fabrics, man-made fabrics started to be used. Rayon which had already been introduced was used as an artificial silk. But by 1939, it was beginning to be replaced – by the stronger and more elastic fabric, Nylon.

Right, escape into style: Fred Astaire and Ginger Rogers in 1933's musical extravaganza *Flying Down To Rio*

Below, Buddy, can you spare a dime? The glittering neon of Broadway illuminates a nightly bread line of the unemployed in New York's Times Square

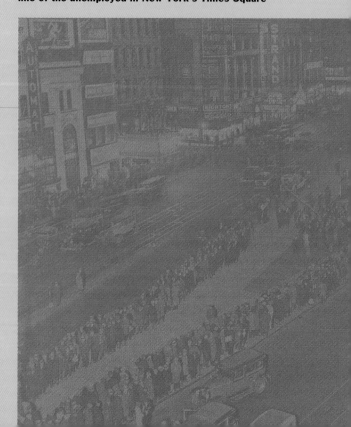

STORY OF CHANEL GABRIELLE 'COCO' CHANEL

FREED WOMEN FROM THE FORMALITY OF EDWARDIAN DRESS AND INTRODUCED THE MODERN VOCABULARY OF WOMEN'S FASHION – JERSEY DRESSES AND SUITS, TROUSERS, THE TRENCH COAT AND 'THE LITTLE BLACK DRESS'.

SHE OPENED HER FIRST SHOP, A MILLINERS, IN DEAUVILLE IN 1913. BUT SOON SHE ADDED SKIRTS, SWEATERS AND THEN ACCESSORIES TO HER RANGE. BY THE END OF THE FIRST WORLD WAR, SHE HAD DEVELOPED THE SIMPLE 'POOR GIRL' LOOK USING JERSEY FABRIC. THIS FREED WOMEN FROM CORSETS. NOT FOR THE LAST TIME, CHANEL HAD CAUGHT THE MOOD OF THE TIMES. SHE MOVED TO PARIS AND DOMINATED THE WORLD OF *HAUTE COUTURE* FOR SIX DECADES. AT THE HEIGHT OF HER CAREER, SHE EMPLOYED 3,500 PEOPLE, AND OWNED A COUTURE HOUSE, A FABRIC MANUFACTURER, MANY PERFUME LABORATORIES AND A COSTUME JEWELLERS.

CHANEL WAS THE FIRST COUTURIÈRE TO FUND HER FASHION EMPIRE ON THE SALES OF PERFUME – CHANEL NO. 5, WHICH WAS INTRODUCED IN 1922. FIVE, CHANEL BELIEVED, WAS HER LUCKY NUMBER.

SHE RETIRED IN 1938, RETURNING TO THE FASHION INDUSTRY IN 1954 WITH THE CLASSIC CHANEL SUIT WITH THE COLLARLESS, CARDIGAN JACKET TRIMMED WITH BRAID AND A MATCHING ELEGANT SKIRT.

'I MAKE FASHIONS THAT WOMEN CAN LIVE IN, BREATHE IN, FEEL COMFORTABLE IN AND LOOK YOUNGER IN,' SAID CHANEL. ONCE AGAIN SHE THREW OUT THE OLD HEAVY, RESTRICTIVE STYLE OF CLOTHING DIOR HAD INTRODUCED. SHE BROUGHT IN A PRACTICAL ELEGANCE WITH HER SIMPLE JERSEY CARDIGAN SUIT. HER USE OF COTTON, RAYON, JERSEY AND HER COSTUME JEWELLERY HELPED UNDERMINE THE ELITIST ATTITUDES OF THE FASHION ESTABLISHMENT AND INFLUENCE THE DRESS OF A BROADER RANGE OF WORKING WOMEN.

SHE WAS AN INTIMATE FRIEND OF PICASSO, COCTEAU AND STRAVINSKY. SHE NEVER MARRIED BUT HER LOVERS INCLUDED THE CREAM OF PARISIAN SOCIETY. HOWEVER, DURING THE OCCUPATION, SHE ALSO ENTERTAINED GERMAN OFFICERS AND VOCALLY SUPPORTED THE VICHY GOVERNMENT. THE FRENCH RESISTANCE, SHE SAID, WERE CRIMINALS. THIS MADE HER HUGELY UNPOPULAR.

Opposite, Gabrielle Chanel
in one of her own suits,
photographed in 1929

An advertisement for Schiaparelli's 'Shocking' range of perfumes and other cosmetics, which actually originated the phrase 'shocking pink'

severe suits and plain black dresses outrageous trimmings that were inspired by the circus, or the military or astrology. And in 1936, while everyone else was using autumnal or pastel colours, Schiaparelli introduced luminous Shocking Pink, which became the trademark of her salon.

While designers such as Alix Barton, later known as Madame Grès, and Victor Stiebel experimented with cellophane, Schiaparelli was drawn to a new fabric called Rhodophane. This was a mixture of cellophane and other synthetic fabrics producing a glass-like material – either clear or frosted. Schiaparelli used it for a line of dress, handbags and shoes. The company who made Rhodophane, Calcombet of Lyon, also provided her with a fabric printed with newspaper clippings. The clippings used were about Schiaparelli, naturally. The fabric was used for blouses, scarves and beachwear. Schiaparelli claimed her inspiration was the hats worn by the women workers in the fish markets of Copenhagen which were made out of newspaper.

Schiaparelli also liked to use unusual and even inappropriate fabrics for their shock value – burlap for day dresses and tweeds for evening wear. She also used zippers in a contrasting colour to the rest of the dress – first in sports wear and later in evening wear. It seemed like a revolutionary act at the time. But Schiaparelli's most shocking experiment was her foray into Surrealism.

Schiaparelli had always liked visual trickery. One of her first commercially successful designs was a black sweater with the white butterfly bow around the neck which was actually a pattern knitted into the sweater. It was spotted by a fashion buyer from an American department store when Schiaparelli wore it to a luncheon party. The buyer immediately ordered forty, with matching skirts. At the time Schiaparelli did not have the facilities to make skirts. But she still found a way to deliver the order.

Elsa Schiaparelli became the most important trend-setter of the decade, both in Paris and in Hollywood. When she moved her house into Chéruit's old salon on the Place Vendôme, her first private customer was Anita Loos, author of *Gentlemen Prefer Blondes*. Schiaparelli also dressed Gloria Swanson, Marlene Dietrich, Norma Shearer and Claudette Colbert.

Famously, Mae West sent a life-size plaster cast of her body in a Venus-de-Milo pose to Paris, so Schiaparelli was able to make her dresses for her movie *Diamond Lil*. Schiaparelli took the cast and, with Surrealist artist Leonor Fini, turned it into the bottles of her perfume 'Shocking'.

Despite the elegant simplicity of her lines – which echoed Chanel's – Schiaparelli would add to her

Right, Marlene Dietrich in a creation by Schiaparelli

Right, a Schiaparelli jacket
with a visual motif by artist
Jean Cocteau

Below, Elsa Sciaparelli's
famous 'lobster dress'
inspired by the surrealist
images of Salvador Dali

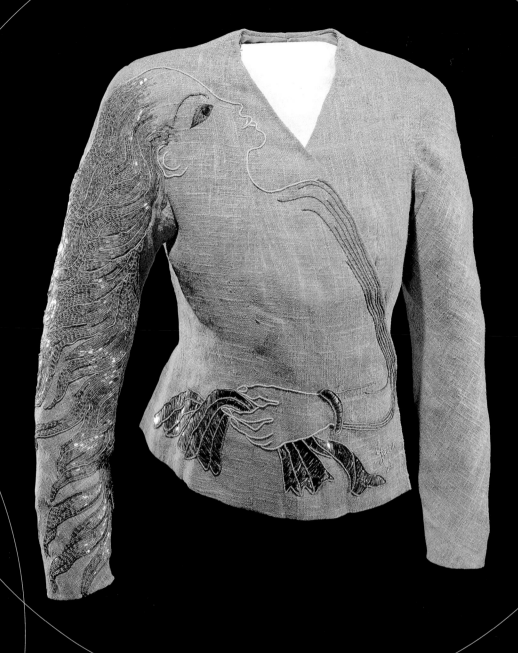

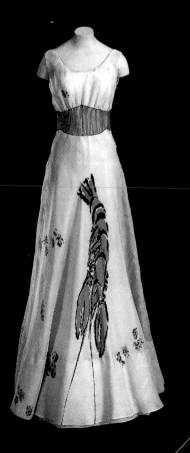

Schiaparelli's knitwear frequently incorporated motifs from African art and Cubism. And when Surrealism came along she usurped that too. In collaboration with Salvador Dali, she produced the Shoe Hat, with a Shocking Pink heel. This was modelled by Dali's wife Gala, who also wore a suit with lips for pockets. The Shoe Hat was bought by fashion leader Mrs Daisy Fellowes.

There were also Chicken-in-a-Basket, Ink-Well, Quill-Pen and Ice-Cream-Cone designs in hats. The Mutton-Chop Hat was designed to be worn with a suit with cutlet motifs embroidered on it. Dali helped with the creation of Schiaparelli's Tear Dress. The fabric has tears printed on it and it was worn with a cape that had real tears in it – an idea that would recur with punk in the 1970s.

Together Dali and Schiaparelli created the Lobster Dress, an organdie dress with giant lobster and sprigs of parsley printed on it.

Schiaparelli produced an evening gown with a large white fabric sea-bird perched on the neck and black evening gloves with gold finger nails attached to the outside. There was a coat with pockets that simulated the drawers of a chest of drawers – a favourite image of Dali's, fluorescent broaches and belts which were fastened with padlocks. Fabrics were printed with elephants, clowns, horses, or incorporated tree bark, straw and glass. She used crazy outsized buttons shaped like bumble bees, peanuts, lollipops, feathers, grasshoppers, paper-weights, guitars and rams' heads. And handbags were shaped like balloons, or lit up or played tunes when they were opened.

Jean Cocteau was another collaborator. He made necklaces with ceramic vegetables, aspirins and metallic insects which were encased in clear plastic and appeared to be crawling around the wearer's neck. Cocteau inspired a jacket with embroidered hands clasped at the waist and gold beading that looked like a woman's hair flowing down one sleeve. Nothing that Dior did a decade later was half as shocking.

During the 1930s, it is estimated that Schiaparelli's *maison* in the Rue Cambon turned over 120 million francs a year. Her twenty-six workrooms employed more than two thousand people.

SURREALISM WAS THE LEADING MOVEMENT IN THE VISUAL ARTS IN THE 1920S AND 1930S. IT GREW OUT OF DADA, AN ANTI-ART MOVEMENT THAT SPRUNG UP DURING WORLD I. BOTH WERE A REJECTION OF EUROPEAN RATIONALISM WHICH SEEN AS THE CAUSE OF THE MASSIVE SLAUGHTER OF WORLD WAR I. WHILE DADA WAS JUST NEGATIVE, SURREALISM WAS FOLLOWING THE TENETS OF FREUD'S PSYCHOANALYSIS AND ALSO SOUGHT TO GIVE POSITIVE EXPRESSION TO SUBCONSCIOUS AND IRRATIONAL THOUGHT. IT BEGAN IN 1924 WHEN POET ANDRÉ BRETON WROTE *THE SURREALIST MANIFESTO.* OTHER POETS NOTABLY PAUL ÉLUARD, FOLLOWED SUIT, BUT SURREALISM MADE ITS MAJOR IMPACT WHEN IT WAS TAKEN UP BY PAINTERS SUCH AS SALVADOR DALI, MAN RAY, MAX ERNST, RENÉ MAGRITTE AND JOAN MIRÓ. THEY PRESENTED AN ALIEN WORLD FULL OF PARADOXES AND STRANGE OBJECTS, OFTEN DEPICTED IN A SUPER REALISTIC WAY.

STYLE AND SOCIETY

The 1930s were the decade that the talkies came into their own. Hair styles and garments created in Hollywood had an immediate effect world-wide. Coco Chanel was the first of the Paris designers to visit the movie mecca in 1929. She was followed by Elsa Schiaparelli, Edward Molyneux, Marcel Rochas, Jeanne Lanvin, Jean Patou and Alix Barton. But Hollywood had its own designers, notably Adrian, Orry-Kelly and Edith Head, all soon to be as famous as anything Paris had to offer.

Adrian designed a white organdie dress, nipped in at the waist, with extended shoulders and ruffled sleeves for Joan Crawford in the 1932 movie *Letty Lynton*. It was so popular that Macy's in New York reported selling over half-a-million copies. It was notable for its padded shoulders, designed to make Joan Crawford's hips look narrower, that dominated the fashion of the early 1940s.

Movies began to exaggerate womanly curves. Shoulders were broadened and shirts draped over the hips. Bias-cut material was used in order to show off the natural shape of a woman's body. But care had to be taken. In 1930, the Hays Office, Hollywood's moral watch-dog, came up with its Production Code, which was intended to crack down on what was seen as moral laxity in films. High on its agenda was the banning of nudity. The eagle eye of Will Hays also settled on revealing and low-cut dresses. So Hollywood designers began show more flesh in other, safer areas and the backless evening dress with a halter neck became the height of fashion.

To draw even more attention to the back, a string of beads or pearls would hang down the spine. An artificial flower or bow would be placed at the base of the spine. Schiaparelli went so far as to add a bustle.

Around the bare shoulders, women would drape an entire foxskin – sometimes even two. Silver fox was extremely fashionable, but the most sought after was white fox.

The movies looked to antiquity for inspiration. Heavy crêpes and dull satins were gathered and pleated so they flowed like the folds in classical Greek sculptures. These techniques had been pioneered by Alix Barton, who draped and moulded jersey, silk and wool. She had begun her career as a sculptor and never worked from sketches. She would create her designs with linen directly on the mannequin so she could follow the line of the woman's body directly.

Men also looked to the movies to see how to dress. George Raft and Humphrey Bogart-style trench coats, with the belt knotted and the collar turned up, became ubiquitous and the soft felt hat, made fashionable by Anthony Eden, gave way to the new snap-brim fedora worn by screen mobsters and gasngsters.

Royalty, as always, was another fashion leader. The dashing young Prince of Wales set the style in formal wear. He adopted the wide-legged American-style trousers that fitted snugly around the hip. The broad Windsor knot he used to tie his tie was widely copied. And he re-introduced the habit of wearing a white waistcoat under his dinner jacket, a style copied by Fred Astaire.

Even when he stood down as King to marry Mrs Wallis Simpson, the two of them always remained trend setters. Wallis Simpson was dressed with elegant simplicity by Molyneux and later Mainbocher, the American Paris-based couturier and ex-editor of French *Vogue*. At the time, she was voted the second-best-dressed woman in the world.

The Duke and Duchess of Windsor at their wedding in France in 1937, her dress is by Mainbocher

Above, MGM Studios'
gown designer Adrian, and
(right) Joan Crawford in
one of his dresses for
Letty Lynton in 1932

Alice Marble sporting shorts at Wimbledon 1933 (left), and some male tennis stars of the period wearing the long flannels that were *de rigueur* for some years to come

The 1930s were a time of great body and health consciousness. Lawn tennis became immensely popular. René Lacoste came up with his famous short-sleeved skirt with the crocodile – called an alligator in the US – motif on it. Professional men players would wear long flannels, until 1932, when Bunny Austin turned up at Forest Hills wearing shorts. Women had gone bare-legged since Schiaparelli designed a culotte dress for Spanish player Lili de Alvarez. This came down to just below the knee and was still far from practical. Then in 1933, Alice Marble appeared at Wimbledon in shorts. Soon after Mrs Fearnely-Whittingstall caused an uproar by appearing without stockings.

Of course, participation in sports was confined to a minority. But designers came up with a line of 'spectator' sports clothes. White skirts and navy blue jackets were thought appropriate for watching tennis or polo. An anchor and ship's wheel motifs were added for those who preferred cruising or watching sailing instead.

For autumn or spring sports, women wore coats and skirt-suits in checked wools or tweed. These outfits were also thought of as appropriate for the popular pastime of 'motoring'. Men were seen in plus-fours, diamond-pattern woollen socks and in single-breasted jackets.

The French beach resorts of Cannes, Biarritz and Le Touquet had come into their own in the 1920s. Coco Chanel had started the fashion of sunbathing, and the invention of Tampax gave women a new freedom in sports – especially swimming.

New elastic yarns – usually rubber combined with silk, cotton or rayon – made swimwear that clung to the body and did not lose it shape when wet. Women bathers abandoned their overskirts and clambered into form-following – though still rather modest – one-piece swim-suits.

The figure hugging one-piece swim suit came into its own during the Thirties

With the craze for suntans, men abandoned the top half of their swimming costumes and the legs of the trunks were cut higher. This caused outrage at first and some swimmers were arrested. But by 1935, topless figure-hugging men's trunks were almost universally accepted.

As the political situation in Europe grew more threatening a new dissenting group grew in society. This was spearheaded by a group of young Bohemian artists and writers who adopted simple, functional clothes, giving the impression that they had more important things to think about than fashion. They wore leather jackets, roll-neck sweaters or open-necked shirts, baggy corduroy trousers and open-toed sandals.

They also grew their hair long – long for the 1930s, at least. And they gave up wearing hats, though some wore berets and women occasionally wore headscarves, peasant style.

Coco Chanel looks on as mannequin Muriel Maxwell models the velvet Watteau suit, in this picture by the top photographer Horst

Modelling Balenciaga at the newly
opened Elizabeth Arden salon at Paris'
Place Vendome, 1939

Meanwhile, within the mainstream, totalitarian propaganda was taking its toll. Following the rise of Hitler, tailored Tyrolean styles became very chic. The military look with square, épauletted shoulders also caught on. But as war approached, fashion began to shy away from military motifs. Couture clothes became nostalgic, looking back towards the safety of the Edwardian era with layers of lace, corset, crinolines – it was practically fancy dress.

There was some fighting spirit though. Some make-up manufacturers such as Cyclax and Helena Rubenstein became positively belligerent with lipsticks named Auxiliary Red and Regimental Red. Schiaparelli launched outfits in Foreign Legion Red and Maginot Line Blue, before she was forced to flee.

America, the home of mass production and ready-to-wear, still felt safe though. But even the casual clothes bought from the stores in the big cities, or from the famous Sears Catalogue were seen in political terms, as if they were somehow some sort of statement about democracy. In 1938, American *Vogue* proclaimed: 'We are clothes-crazy people, we boast that our shop-girls looks as attractive as our social butterflies, that our jerk-water towns tilt their hats at the same angle as out big cities; we're even a little smug about being called, as we frequently are, the best-dressed women in the world. Actually, it isn't so much that we are the best dressed – it is that more of us are well dressed. A handful of top-flight Frenchwomen easily outstrip us in creating and wearing clothes, but collectively, en masse, our 40,000,000 adult females are better dressed, more fashion-conscious than any others on the face of the earth.

'But, you say, these are commonplaces. And so they are, the commonplaces of mass production and mass distribution; the ordinary week-day tale of great businesses that cater to the great mass of American woman; of a nation that has grown strong because it believed that commonplace needs were important. Perhaps the founding fathers would be surprised if they should wake today, to see out literal interpretation of their theories, to see a democracy of government achieve also the only democracy of fashion in the world. They might be surprised, but we do not believe that they would be displeased.'

One final, remarkable, thing happened in fashion before the world was engulfed in war. In 1939, Chanel showed a wasp-waisted full-skirt suit in stark contradiction of her usual style. Lelong too, featured cinched waists and full skirts that same season. Molyneux and Mainbocher both showed full dirndl skirts.

Vogue said: 'The only thing you must have is a tiny waist, held in if necessary by super-light-weight boned and laced corsets.'

But the practicalities of war intervened and the wasp-waist disappeared amongst the chaos, not to be seen again until Christian Dior stunned the world with it eight long years later.

'Lelong binds up a small
waist, runs a navy scarf
round your neck and calls
it a bodice' –
UK *Vogue*, 1939

Coco Chanel in 1929, in one of her own suits, typical of her fashion break-throughs which so captivated Christian Dior early on in his career

DIOR ON THE 1930S

DIOR WORKED FOR PIGUET, ONE OF THE SMALLER COUTURIERS, DURING THE 1930S. HIS TECHNIQUE WAS VERY BASIC AND HE DEPENDED ON SIMPLICITY TO GIVE HIS OUTFITS THEIR ELEGANCE.

COCO CHANEL WAS ONE OF DIOR'S IDOLS. SHE AND MADELAINE VIONNET, HE BELIEVED, WERE THE FOUNDERS OF MODERN FASHION. HE ADMIRED CHANEL'S ELEGANT WIT AND THE WAY SHE ABOLISHED *FROU FROU* AND EDWARDIAN OVERDRESSING.

DIOR HAD NO TIME FOR SCHIAPARELLI. HE DETESTED HER CREATIONS, CONDEMNING THEM AS LOUD AND VULGAR. WORST OF ALL, HE DESPISED HER ATTEMPT TO TRANSLATE SURREALISM INTO FASHION.

AN ANGLOPHILE, DIOR PREFERRED MOLYNEUX AND HIS SMALL, SEVERE DRESSES. WITH MOLYNEUX, DIOR SAID, 'NOTHING IS EVER INVENTED, EVERYTHING SPRINGS FROM SOMETHING ELSE. HIS IS THE STYLE THAT HAS MOST INFLUENCED ME.'

MOLYNEUX WAS A PERFECTIONIST AND, AS AN ENGLISHMAN, THE MASTER OF THE UNDERSTATEMENT. YET DIOR WAS A

ROMANTIC AND HIS CLOTHES WOULD EXPLODE WITH EXTRAVAGANCE IN A WAY THAT MOLYNEUX WOULD HAVE FOUND VULGAR. MOLYNEUX ALSO BELIEVED IN THE STEADY EVOLUTION OF FASHION. DIOR CRAVED THE IMPACT OF A REVOLUTION.

DIOR ONLY KNEW MOLYNEUX SLIGHTLY IN THE 1930S, ALTHOUGH DIOR'S APARTMENT WAS ALMOST OPPOSITE MOLYNEUX' COUTURE HOUSE. MOLYNEUX' INFLUENCE ON DIOR CAME LARGELY VIA PIERRE BALMAIN, A DESIGNER AT MOLYNEUX, WHO WORKED ALONGSIDE DIOR AT LELONG. HOWEVER, DIOR AND MOLYNEUX BECAME FIRM FRIENDS IN LATER LIFE.

Schiaparelli's very whimsical smoking glove, fashioned from red suede with safety matches in the cuff and a striking board on the wrist

FASHION ON THE

RATION

41

'While we are wearing rayon,' lamented American Vogue, 'the Frenchwoman 'is wearing yards of silk.'

WHILE WE ARE WEARING RAYON, THE FRENCHWOMAN IS WEARING YARDS OF SILK.'

In 1938, as the clouds of war gathered over Europe, the couturiers' full-skirted ballgowns were shipped off to America and shorter, more skimpy skirts came into fashion in Europe. Elsa Schiaparelli, inevitably, bucked the trend with a long skirt that could be hitched up, so the woman could walk. She also introduced huge pockets to women's garments so they did not have to carry a handbag.

Paris fell to the Germans in June 1941. But, although the French suffered a great deal under the occupation, the couturiers never experienced the wartime shortages of their counterparts in the UK or America. 'While we are wearing rayon,' lamented American *Vogue*, the Frenchwoman 'is wearing yards of silk.'

A coupon system was introduced, but the Paris fashion houses were given special fabric allowances and were allowed to sell their clothes outside the coupon system. There were some restrictions of course. No badge styles that aped French uniforms were allowed. However, the couturiers established a second front. They realised that the more material they used, the less was left for the Germans. The more labour they used, the fewer people would be taken as forced labour into the German factories.

The more the Germans attempted to restrict their output, the more defiant the fashion houses became. Flamboyant fashion became the French woman's way of saying that, although her country had been occupied, its spirit had not been broken. Being coquettish was the one form of resistance left. Colours became glaring, skirts shortened, jackets lengthened and hats flamboyantly decorated. Some stood 18 inches high. Schiaparelli's Parisian house which continued while Schiaparelli in person was exiled in the US, produced a line of hats with small crowns and upturned brims - in deliberate defiance of the Vichy government who wanted its supporters to wear berets.

Women who could not afford to buy from the couturiers followed suit. They added colourful patches to old clothes to re-enliven rather than mend them. They too turned to large hats to lift their spirits. When the pre-war stock of material had run out, they used plaited straw. When that ran out, they used coloured paper. And they found other ways around the regulations. Millinery shops were restricted to one yard of material for a beret, one for a turban and one for a brimmed sailor hat. But if you combined the three together in one hat you could use three yards of material. The hats were counter-balanced by huge wedge platform shoes with soles made from cork or wood.

For the first six months of World War II, it was possible to get clothes from Paris, even expensive ones, in London and New York. But gradually the price increased by 25 per cent and clothes became more difficult to obtain.

Right, a *Vogue* advert from 1939, with a masculine-influenced skirt described in the blurb as being 'built for bestriding bicycles'

Propaganda becomes you: a 'No Idle Talk' warning, with the possibility of German agents lurking at every corner, is featured around the veil of a hat

A grey wool divided skirt, built for bestriding bicycles; deep pockets swallow your hand-bag necessities (£3 13s.); blue angora blouse (59s. 6d.) Jaeger; cushion-soled brogues, Pinet

1941

An example of how good Utility clothes could look is this perfectly tailored suit made in wool by Dorville, 1946

From the very beginning of the war, the demand for uniforms caused fabric shortages in Britain. Material normally employed in making curtains or upholstery was seconded to the garment industry and by 1940 'shoddy' – a coarse reprocessed woollen cloth – was in widespread use.

Although of poor quality, clothing was not scarce. But the industry had to be regulated to release valuable labour and factory space for the manufacture of armaments and munitions. In May 1941, Minister of Labour Ernest Bevin introduced the Utility scheme which controlled half, then 85 per cent of cloth manufacture, fixing its price, quality and colour. Only monochrome colours, such as Flag Red and Victory Blue, were used to cut down on wastage. Utility cloth had to be used for Utility clothing, which was sold at a fixed price and not subject to purchase tax. Clothes rationing

Two of the first Utility dresses designed by Norman Hartnell and launched in 1942. Each dress was available in twelve different colours 'to avoid dullness'

began on 1 June 1941. Each adult received 66 coupons a year. But this was quickly reduced to 48. In 1945, it was cut further to just 36, though extra coupons were available on the flourishing black market. By a weird quirk of the regulations, surplus margarine coupons could be spent on clothing and some well-to-do housewives would buy extra coupons off their charladies. 2s 6d (12p) was the going rate – which was 60 cents at the 1941 exchange rate.

Eighteen coupons were needed to buy a woman's tweed suit; fourteen for a coat; eleven for a jacket; and eleven for a woollen dress. A skirt was seven; a blouse four; a waistcoat or jumper five. Handkerchiefs needed two coupons each. Shoes were seven, but you were able to save two coupons if you bought shoes with wooden soles. However, great care had to be taken when drying them out

when it rained as in the rain they would split easily.

There were not many styles to choose from. Wedge heels and peep toes were popular, but the shoes queues were so bad women sometimes had to queue for a ticket to get into the queue. The fashion for outdoor wedges, or platform shoes with ankle straps, persisted after the war. 'French straw' was a particular colour in summer.

A man's overcoat needed sixteen coupons, a shirt eight, underpants four. The wartime President of the Board of Trade, Hugh Dalton, advised men not in uniform to go to work without a collar, tie or socks to save material. Dalton himself did not buy a new suit for the duration of the war.

It was unpatriotic to sleep with pyjamas or a nightdress. But women whose husbands were away wore thick, warm Viyella pyjamas, which they could also wear around the house in day-time.

A fine example of outdoor wedge shoes from 1945 with the platform soles made of cork

and 5,000 tons of raw material, which could be used to make 2,000,000 battle dresses or clothe 500,000 soldiers from head to foot, including underwear, boots and greatcoat!'

At first, points were allotted to the garments regardless of quality, but in the autumn of 1941, the Utility Scheme was extended to control the quality and price of clothing. Detailed specifications were drawn up and 85 per cent of clothing had to be made to Utility standard. To organise clothing manufacture in Britain, Margaret Havinden, a director of Crawford's advertising agency, had brought together the leading couturiers in Britain in 1941. Their first task was to co-ordinate an export drive. Led by Edward Molyneux, the group formed and became the Incorporated Society of London Fashion Designers. ISLFD members included Norman Hartnell, Hardy Amis, Digby Morton, Victor Stiebel, Bianca Mosca, Peter Russell and Champcommunal at Worth. Later, Angèle Delange, Lachasse, Michael, John Cavanagh, Mattli, Michael Sherard, Charles Creed and Ronald Paterson joined. Fifteen per cent of all materials were set aside for export. Eighty British models were sent off to the US and 'Buy British' shops were opened in New York.

This export drive continued after the end of the war. In 1946, the ISLFD put on an exhibition at the Victoria & Albert Museum called 'Britain Can Make It'. Disappointed visitors soon discovered that most of the garments on display were for export only and disgruntled fashion buyers renamed the exhibition 'Britain Can't Have It'.

Sadly, the line was not wildly popular even abroad. While classic British fabrics such as Harris tweed brought in much needed dollars, no one really considered British design of the post-war austerity period a patch on that of Paris or the new generation of designers in New York.

More examples of the Berketex Utility range designed by Norman Hartnell, here in June 1943

Those in the armed services or other occupations where they were issued with uniforms were made to surrender some of their coupons. A nurse had to give up ten coupons; a policewoman six. Individuals were also urged to give up coupons voluntarily to help with the war effort. One of the posters of the time explained that: 'If everybody took a pair of scissors and cut out and gave to salvage one coupon, it would release 8,000 workers

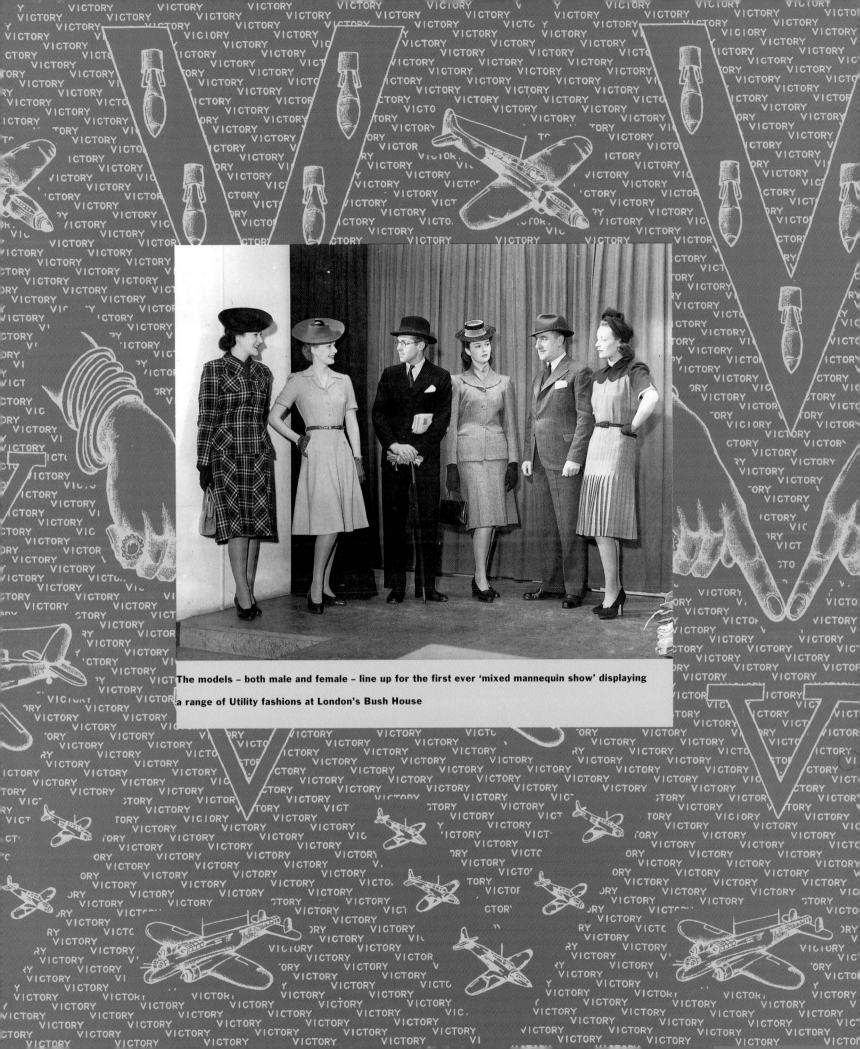

The models – both male and female – line up for the first ever 'mixed mannequin show' displaying a range of Utility fashions at London's Bush House

ISSUED BY THE BOARD OF TRADE

These darns save clothes says Mrs. SEW-and-SEW

BEST DARNS FOR SOCKS. Use fine wool. Be sure to weave your needle under and over evenly, going well beyond thin part round hole. Leave loops at either end to allow for shrinking.

NEATEST DARN FOR TEAR in a suit, coat, or woollen frock. Tack paper behind tear to keep it in position. Catch the edges together with fine matching cotton. Unravel some threads from seams of garment, and darn across and across the tear with fine even stitches. Press well.

STRONGEST DARN FOR LEATHER. For tear in glove or jacket, buttonhole all round, then buttonhole the two edges together.

FLEXIBLE DARN FOR KNITTEDS. Begin with straight rows as for socks, but weave in and out crosswise, on the diagonal.

free DARNING LEAFLETS

with clear diagrams of all the most useful darns, including invisible repair for stocking ladder. Send a card to the Public Relations Dept., Board of Trade, Millbank, London, S.W.1, asking for the Darning Leaflets. Free and post free.

join a class . . .

Your local Evening Institute, Technical College or Women's Organisation is probably running a Make-Do and Mend Class. Ask at your Citizens' Advice Bureau.

Make Do and Mend

The British government's 'make do and mend' campaign encouraged women to cut up old clothes and re-style them. The campaign was headed by a cosy government publicity lady called Mrs Sew-and-Sew. She explained how to turn two dish clothes into a sort of jersey and an old men's overcoat into a tweed coat and skirt. Old cotton dresses were made into aprons. Pre-war hats were refurbished by adding ribbons, sequins, beads, coloured cord, bits of net or braid. Newspapers, magazines and the radio also offered hints on 'make do and mend'. Information was given on how to make skirts out of old trousers, how to reverse collars, how to make clothes for babies out of pillowcases and how to unravel sweaters and knit something new.

Knitting was all important as woollen garments required more coupons than rayon - or even silk, if you could get it. There were fuel shortages and wool kept out the cold. Besides knitting was something you could do to keep yourself busy and while away long nights in the air-raid shelter.

The most popular design was, of course, the Victory jumper. It had a V-neck and was covered in V-motifs. Enterprising women also turned their skills towards non-rationed goods. Blankets were dyed and made into coats. A little bit of lace was added to a pillowcase to make a blouse. Odd or extra pieces of knitting were patchworked into warm winter waistcoats. Old curtains were turned into skirts. Net curtains and butter muslin were used to make wedding dresses. And parachute silk became lingerie and evening wear. 'Use it up, wear it out, make it do or do without,' became the slogan of the day.

Two showgirls from the Prince Of Wales Theatre in London, 1941, wearing dresses they have made from lace curtains

A 'Make and Mend' exhibition in November 1942 included this lumber jacket made from a man's blazer and the little girl's jumper fashioned from 'a lady's unpicked cardigan'

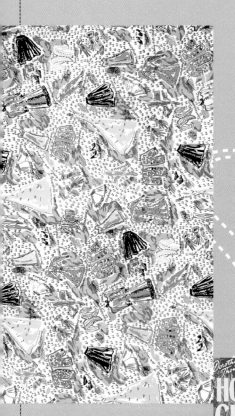

This piece of Utility fabric had '66' and 'sixty six coupons' featured in the design, referring to the rationed limit in force

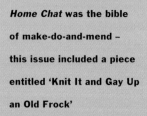

Home Chat was the bible of make-do-and-mend – this issue included a piece entitled 'Knit It and Gay Up an Old Frock'

Of course, not everyone had the time or the skills to 'make do and mend'. And dressmakers advertised: 'Last season's dresses coats etc made to look new.'

Make do and mend even affected royalty. King George VI wore his pre-war suits throughout the duration. New cuffs for his shirts were made from material cut from the shirt-tails. Otherwise he would appear on public occasions in uniform – usually naval uniforms as he had served in the Royal Navy during World War I. The Duke of Windsor, despite his Nazi sympathies, also did his bit. He was seen wearing a tartan suit made for his father George V in the 1890s. This started a trend in the US. Soon it was fashionable to be seen in a tartan dinner jacket, tartan cummerbund and even tartan swimming trunks.

In America, there was not actually an official 'make do and mend' policy, but Sears praised American housewives for doing their bit on the home front by running up clothes with the aid of *McCall's* patterns and a Sears sewing machine.

Women were also asked to give up certain luxuries in order to help the war effort. In New York, there was a campaign to collect fur coats to make fur-lined vests for the merchant sailors on the Atlantic convoys.

BOARD OF TRADE

Those old white flannels can save you coupons

This Kent girl made her bra and knickers from the parachute of a crashed German pilot. Embroiderd on it was 'ME 109' (the fighter plane) 'Bridge Farm, 1940' and a drawing of the Luftwaffe cross insignia

ite flannels are not being worn much these days—
ity to let them lie idle when there's so much
can be done with the material. Here are
e suggestions from Make-do and Mend classes.
if there isn't an idea for you amongst them.

g COUPONS SAVED

or

3 COUPONS SAVED

FOUR JACKETS FOR A NEW BABY
—were made in magyar style from one worn pair of white flannels. Saving 2 coupons each.

SHORTS FOR A SMALL BOY
—were shown at another class. Not easy to cut correctly without practice—but there's an expert at each class to help.

SKIRT FOR A SCHOOLGIRL
—was another success chosen and the ... ...red style ... over ... ough mar ... ...ke suspender st ...

or
4 COUPONS SAVED

36 37 38 39 40 41 42 43 44 45 46 47 48 49 50 51 52 53 54 55 56 57 58 59 60 61 62 63

1942

A Cecil Beaton picture
from the Board of Trade
launch of Utility clothes by
the Incorporated Society
of Fashion Designers

The ubiquitous Utility label
– it stood for Civilian
Clothing 1941 – to be
found in all Board of Trade
approved garments during
and after the War

In 1942, a series of Making of Clothes (Restrictions) Orders were introduced. These were to specify the maximum width and length of skirts and restricted the number of pleats, pockets and button-holes – all in order to save fabric. The use of trimmings were curtailed. Embroidery and sequin decoration banned. The total amount of cloth in each garment was strictly fixed and the number of new styles that could be introduced was restricted. The British Standards Institution was also brought in fix sizes, so that any alternations could be kept to an absolute minimum.

Under these regulations, the ISLFD created a line of austerity clothes. Members were asked to design for four basic items – an afternoon dress, a dress for office work, a coat and a suit. Thirty-two were selected for production. They were practical and warm, but saved as much fabric and labour as was possible. They were approved under the Utility Clothing Scheme by the President of the Board of Trade, Hugh Dalton, in February 1942, and stamped 'CC41'.

The Utility look actually developed from the severe masculine look introduced by Schiaparelli and Rochas in the late 1930s, though perhaps the most obvious precursor was Joan Crawford's dress in the 1932 movie *Letty Lynton* which was designed by Adrian. This was the origin for the square-shouldered, short-skirted look that the Utility designers and, later, American designers working to Limiting Order L-85 followed. It is ironic that, although wartime restrictions were in force to make every possible saving in the raw materials, women still had padded shoulders.

Long gone were the lavish, bias-cut, mid-calf tea-dresses of the pre-war period. Dresses were much simpler shirt-waisters with few buttons down the front and small, reversed cuffs. A slim belt defined the waist. The skirt was sparingly cut and only lightly pleated or gathered.

The most popular outfit of the time was the *tailleur*, the two-piece suit. This gave women a very serious, business-like look and also reflected the uniforms that many women found themselves in. Jackets were square-shouldered, plain and slightly bloused. Skirts were straight, narrow-hipped and reached just over the knee. Colours were red and black, burgundies, bottle greens and dusky blues. The look was functional, even militaristic. Buttons were rationed so there were none on the cuffs and a plain shirt blouse was worn under the jacket. The Utility range of hats also had a distinct military look, based on caps and berets.

Mock suits were also in demand. These were dresses made to look like a two-piece suit with a jacket – but they required fewer coupons.

The regulations were strictly applied and those caught trying to get round them were fined heavily. In 1943, Lady Astor asked some American friends to send some clothes over for her. The clothes were intercepted and she was fined £50 – ten times the price of a Utility suit.

Even ladies underwear was regulated – no lace, no embroidery, no frills. Three years after the end of the war, a dressmaker in London was arrested for embroidering flowers on lingerie. This was viewed as an unpatriotic waste.

However, it was possible to buy those fabrics and garments produced outside the Utility scheme. But the 15 per cent of non-Utility garments followed very much the same design, only they were of better quality and finish. This was largely because, in the atmosphere of austerity, ostentation was looked upon with suspicion.

However, non-regulated items became scarce and prices were high – not least because purchase tax was levied on all non-coupon items. A coat and skirt which cost 14 guineas – £14.70 – before the war rose to £42 and a 25-shilling (£1.25) pre-war nightie would cost £13. These price rises were way above the 31 percent rise in the cost of living.

The first item to disappear completely in Britain was silk stockings. They vanished from the shops in December 1940. The silk was needed to make parachutes. Women were told that manufacturers had rayon, cotton and woollen alternatives. Thick rayon crêpe stockings in bright colours such as apple green, rose and lilac were available to start with. But by 1942, hosiery was in such short supply

that women were reduced to wearing socks with dresses and suits. This led to the bobby sox of the late forties.

Trousers also became popular as another way around the shortage of stockings. Those who were more enterprising applied Cyclax Stocking-less cream or sun-tan lotions to their legs and drew a seamline down the back their leg with an eyebrow pencil. No wonder British women were delighted when the GIs turned up with nylons.

Those women who knew someone in a parachute regiment often got a length of parachute silk to make into undies – even though this was a crime punishable by imprisonment. And the women who were wearing silk underwear gave themselves away because they rustled when they moved.

Undertakers were popular with the women too. They had plentiful supplies of muslin, which was used to line coffins.

Most people accepted the shortages cheerfully though. The Board of Trade produced posters in order to explain: 'Corsets become parachutes and chin-straps; lace curtains become sand-fly netting; toilet preparations become anti-gas ointments; combs become eyeshields.'

So the privations of war were accepted as part of the struggle against Hitler and the Nazis.

"The surest way," Matilda said,
"To give the Axis knocks
Is letting your suspenders out
And wearing shorter socks.

The shorter sock saves labour, dear
And tons of precious wool—
Like General Alexander's head,
It's practical and cool.

So do not search for longer hose—
Forego those extra inches!
With shorter socks make Hitler feel
Just where his own shoe pinches!"

Leg make-up took the place of silk stockings – here a Hollywood starlet demonstrates how to draw a good seam-line with the aid of an eyebrow pencil

Wolsey

WOMEN'S HOSE OUTLOOK FOR 1946

- 600 MILLION
- 500 MILLION
- 400 MILLION
- 360,000,000 NYLONS
- 300 MILLION
- 240,000,000 RAYON
- 200 MILLION
- 100 MILLION
- 48,000,000 COTTON & WOOL

A model decorates this chart illustrating the American statistics for nylon stockings – as opposed to cotton, wool and rayon – for 1946

During the early years of the war in Europe, America was still the land of plenty. Before the fall of France, many American women thought that it was their patriotic duty to support democracy and buy Parisian designs. After the Occupation, there was a vogue for all things British.

After December 1941 and America's entry into the war, the US began to suffer restrictions too. There was a ban on the import of Japanese silk. In 1942, Sears offered a domestic rayon raincoat, to replace the imported silk ones that they could no longer obtain. The military had commandeered all remaining stocks of silk to make parachutes.

For hosiery, nylon took over. Nylons first went on sale at the beginning of the war in Wilmington, Delaware, with the slogan 'Halve stocking bills without loss of glamour.' Nylon was much more hard wearing – the average pair of silk stockings only lasted 130 hours. But Nylon itself was soon required for military purposes. And although nylon stockings had already appeared in the 1940 Sears catalogue, they had disappeared three years later.

American women took to wearing leg make-up or cotton stockings. Sears advised women to keep their rayon stockings for 'furlough' dates.

Cosmetics

At the outbreak of war, the British government tried to ban make-up - but relented when they realised how this would damage morale. Nevertheless, cosmetics companies such as Yardley had to have their factories turned over to the production of aircraft parts and sea-water purifiers. The output of cosmetics fell to a quarter of their pre-war output.

Some manufacturers were refilling old lipstick tubes. Few women had more than two lipsticks to last the war and some even used beetroot juice to stain lips. The WAAF issued its own lipstick but it was as dry as dust and had a bitter taste. Women would stand around with their mouths open waiting for it to dry and it ended up looking like greasepaint. Women were told to use potato flesh, lemon juice or egg white to tone the skin. Egg yolk instead of shampoo and vegetable oil could be used as foundation. However, as food was rationed, this advice was far from practical.

In the US, the War Production Board conducted a survey to see which cosmetics were vital to wartime morale. Lipstick, rouge and face powder came top and bath oil was also essential. For British women this would have been a luxury: in 1943, bath water was limited to 5 inches, no matter how many shared. These regulations were mostly followed by a patriotic public.

THE IDEA WAS TO FREEZE FASHIO
DATE BEFORE IT WAS WORN OUT

A stylish pair of waterproof velvet overboots – 'white for the black-out, bordered with white velvet'

These white 'black-out' buttonholes from Harrods featured in the November '39 *Vogue* were luminous so they shone at night

Although American *Vogue* encouraged sensible fashions for the war, they were also reminded the fashion industry of its role in maintaining morale. Luckily, the 'tubbable' cotton frock was already in fashion in the US and there was no shortage of soap. British women had to live with a soap ration of just four ounces a month – white gloves and white or pastel blouses quickly went out of fashion.

At the beginning of the war, actress Ruby Miller had suggested that British women wear light coloured clothing in the blackout in order to avoid accidents. But this soon proved impractical and women preferred luminous pins and brooches, often in floral designs.

By the summer of 1942, Limiting Order L-85 was brought in, in America. These were a less stringent version of the British Utility measures. The aim was to cut domestic fabric production by 15 per cent, saving 40-50 million pounds of wool alone.

The idea was to freeze fashion, so nothing became out of date before it was worn out. Consequently, there was little perceptible change in fashion between 1941 and 1946. The industry itself noted the exigencies of the moment.

'It is innocent to think that ingenuity on the part of our designers and producers can surmount every shortage and triumph over every curtailment,' wrote The Fashion Group in 1942. 'Fashion will not be "as usual," any more than life, business, transportation, or taxes. They face a two-fold responsibility. This industry has existed on the very nature of change, and now change is limited... not only by Government Orders... but by the need to avoid obsolescence and waste at all costs. Yet in the face of all this it is their job to keep the flame of creative ability bright, and to keep alive a respect for all we mean by quality.'

The king of luxury fashion, Stanley Marcus of Neiman-Marcus in Dallas, Texas, was summoned to Washington twenty days after the Japanese attack on Pearl Harbour to sell the new restrictions to the American people.

Like the British regulations, the L-85 orders specified the amount of fabric that could go into a garment. It fixed the lengths and widths of jackets, skirts and trousers, and the number of buttons, pleats and the amount of trimming. Coat hoods, patch pockets, cuffs, double yokes and anything that required 'fabric on fabric' was banned. Skirts could be no more than six feet in circumference, hems could be no more than two inches and belts a maximum of two inches wide. Resourceful young designers made sporty suits with short, narrow skirts and jackets not exceeding 25 inches in length. Men's three-piece suits lost their vests. The jackets lost their pocket flaps; the pants their pleats and cuffs. Stanley Marcus presented these new designs as patriotic chic.

As apparel consultant to the War Production Board, he told fashion designers that it was their patriotic duty to produce clothes that would remain in fashion for several seasons, releasing vital factory space and labour for war work. But buying clothes was not to be discouraged completely.

An advertisement in the US *Vogue* in 1942 for cotton stockings by Milena

Zoot Suits, Wide Boys and Zazous

In the US Black and Hispanic teenagers in Harlem and Los Angeles did not feel they had much to do with the war. They pioneered the zoot suit, an unpatriotically wasteful style. Jackets reached the knees with huge shoulder pads, the trouser waist reached the chest, the crouch hug low, the waist was pleated and legs wide. It was infact everything the L-85 regulations said it should not be. It was topped with long hair, a broad-brimmed hat, pointed shoes, a huge tie, and a long chain. It was so offensive to servicemen that some zoot-suiters were beaten up while the police looked the other way and some states considered outlawing it. But the fashion was picked up by the underworld as the Drape Shape jackets could conceal guns. It was also adopted by stars like Danny Kaye and Frank Sinatra. English Teddy boys adapted the 'drape', with an Edwardian feel, adding drain-pipe trousers, a waistcoat and bootlace tie. Many were appalled, but *Tailor and Cutter's* editor John Taylor traced these fashions back to a Savile Row tailor, F.P. Scholte of the nineteenth century, who had adapted it from Guard's officer's coats.

Gangsters and film-stars also made broad fish-tail ties fashionable. The most famous came from a shop in

Black teenagers in their zoot suits at the famous Savoy Ballroom, Harlem, in the late 1930s

New York, run by 'Countess Mara'— not a countess, but
her mother was a baroness and she claimed to be a
descendant of Tintoretto. Her pictorial and hand
painted ties cost up to $20 and had a CM with a crown
on them. They were instantly recognisable and
strangers wearing CM ties would greet each other,
forging a secret brotherhood.

Although the Drape look was mainstream in America, in
Britain it never caught on, they were proud of their
tailoring and well cut suits. However, the underworld
developed its own style. 'Spivs' — or black-market
racketeers — wore flashy suits with wide lapels. They
were known as wide boys , wearing wide chalk-striped
suits originally worn by Edward VIII, but which had
fallen out of favour since the abdication. This was
augmented with kipper ties, a 'trilby' hat and a thin
moustache, in contrast to RAF handlebar moustaches
favoured by city types.

In Paris, spivs' equivalents were called zazous. They
wore drop-shouldered, long jackets with tight
trousers, the women wore striped stockings, short
skirts and square-shouldered fur coats. Both men and

A sinister-looking zazou in 1944

women wore dark glasses and carried umbrellas.

With the end of the war, recriminations began about
who had collaborated with Germans. Suddenly the style
was unfashionable and only seen in second-hand shops.

Making clothes from food sacks became something of a craze in Forties America, when the grain producers began changing their previously drab sacks for new brightly coloured cotton bags

Left, General Dwight D. Eisenhower, the Allied Supreme Commander who helped popularise the wind-cheater, here with Major General Troy Middleton who is wearing a classic battledress jacket

'Many a woman with the best intentions in the world thinks she is doing her bit, making a noble sacrifice, by refusing to buy any new clothes during the duration,' American *Vogue* told its readers. 'But so complex is our economic life that this very act of self-denial may cause injury to the delicately adjusted gears which must continue to mesh if that great machine is to continue to function, if that great machine is to swing into the mightiest armaments production line of all time.

'Arms and munitions, boats and planes are made by workers, who are paid in the money that comes from defense bonds and taxes. A sizable part of these taxes comes from the clothing industry – in peacetime, the second largest of our country. The makers of fashionable shoes and hats, gloves and bags, of dresses and coats and suits – all these makers are operating with full government approval. Whatever is on sale in a shop is there to be bought, with the Goverment's full permission. Refusal to buy only helps to dislocate the public economy.'

The Sears catalogue, being the invaluable guide to fashion trends, still continued to carry 1940s' classics – including the camel's hair boy coat, the reversible raincoat, the twin Shetland sweater sets, the shirt-waister dress, saddle shoes and the Chesterfield coat with the velvet collar that even won a Coty award in 1943. The blouses and hats imitated uniforms. The 'battledress top' or the 'Eisenhower wind-cheater' were also popular. Items like the Tank Corps berets and peaked caps with a glitter on them helped American women who were not in uniform believe that they too were backing the war effort.

Rubber was needed for the war, so rubber girdles were banned in the US. One manufacturer went back to producing whale-bone corsets, but largely women went without girdles for the duration.

Zipper factories were also turned over to armament production, therefore fastenings were banned. Sequins, too, were considered inessential and were also restricted.

Order L-116 banned any embroidery and order M-217 aimed to conserve leather and limited shoes to six colours. The maximum height of heels was fixed at 1 inch and American women were advised to buy comfortable wedgies or low heels to walk in to conserve gasoline. There was petrol rationing in Britain too, but British woman were allowed heels up to 2 inches.

Even in America there were shortages. The Sears catalogue would turn up with 'sorry, not available' stamped over items with increasing regularity. Shoppers were advised to buy only high-quality merchandise which would last. Fashion magazines stressed classic lines that would stay in fashion for several seasons, while regular women's magazines ran features on the proper way to wash and take care of clothing.

With Paris behind enemy lines, the American designers came into their own. Norman Norrell, Charles James and Claire McCardell were all very influential. The big six stores in New York – Bonwit Teller, Saks Fifth Avenue, Sally Migrim, Hattie Carnegie, Bergdorf Goodman and Jay Thorpe all held fashion shows featuring American designs twice daily.

Norman Norell went into the ready-to-wear market where he tailored waistless jersey shifts that reduced the use of fabric by 50 per cent. But it was Claire McCardell who really pioneered the American look. She worked in gingham, calico, demin and even striped mattress ticking. Her 1942 Popover dress became a classic – a wrap-around denim overall, which sold 75,000 in a year and remained fashionable into the 1950s.

casual clothes. The demand for 'play clothes' grew during the war and many people found their day clothes – a uniform – was supplied by the Pentagon.

Designers combed the country for American ideas. Ready-to-wear designers turned to cheap and cheerful sources of inspiration and came up with 'Mexican' peasant blouses, polka-dot 'Pioneer' dresses, boldly checked 'Country and Western' skirts and the tough demin jeans that the California firm Levi-Strauss & Co had made since 1890, now began their relentless expansion into everyday fashion. Denim appeared in playclothes and the sportswear pages of the Sears catalogue featured slacks.

Dallas, Texas, which was traditionally the home of sportswear, found itself competing with Los Angeles. During the war, eighty-five per cent of California's output of sportswear ended up in the large East Coast stores and manufacturers were happy to produce exclusive lines for shops who placed such large orders. The most famous Californian manufacturers of that time were Cole of California and Catalina Knitting Mills, under Edgar Stewart. Classic causal clothes were made by Koret of California, White Stag and Pendleton, who had began by producing Indian blankets in Oregon in 1909. The West Coast style of casual dressing took another leap forward in 1943 when Mary Lewis, the vice president of Best & Company, became the fashion director of Sears.

Sportswear was a fashion that had come from the university campuses. This was one way that the students could appear both conservative as well as fashionable. It began in the 1930s, when college stores began carrying sports clothes, then really took off with the launch of the successful *Mademoiselle* magazine. This being the very first magazine for both young college and career women, in 1935.

American college students in 1940s California. Note the bobby sox (on her) and his Shetland sweater and light flannels

She particularly hated the wedge and platform shoes that had balanced out the square-shouldered wartime look. In 1944, she commissioned ballet slipper manufacturer Capezio to come up with a more rugged version that she would be able to wear outdoors – ballet slippers, conveniently, fell outside US wartime restrictions.

Dorothy Shaver, later president of Lord and Taylor, was particularly active in encouraging young American designers in the area of sports and

Initially the style was very British with 'Brooks Brothers' Shetland sweaters, men's flannel slacks, pleated flannel skirts, fly fronted gabardine and double-breasted camel's-hair polo coats, tweed balmacaans and tailored suits, white-and-brown spectator pumps and saddle shoes. But by the 1940s, the campuses were generating their own styles, combining separates and sportswear to make a college look. By 1949, this casual college look accounted for 30 per cent of the industry, *Life* said. Schiaparelli, in New York, was full of praise.

'It's amazing what America does with reasonably priced clothes, especially sports clothes,' she said. 'So much taste.'

In Britain too, sportswear – especially tennis or golfing clothes – became fashion items in their own right. But that was largely to get more wear of out pre-war clothes that would otherwise not have seen the light of day during the conflict.

American casual clothes were simply downright patriotic. The Sears catalogue was full of sailor suits and red, white and blue outfits. Captions were suitably jingoistic: 'It's the American Way... to Live in a Dress with Jacket.' There was even the 'Miss America' polo coat.

Other looks were a 'sunny California fashion' or incorporated 'Californian style'. Some were 'Hawaiian inspired'. Shoes were huaraches said to be 'inspired by Mexico'. The Moc-inette was a 'frontier fashion', like a Native American moccasin with fringes. And there were 'cactus-country style' shoes, made in tooled leather with 'all the tang and dash of the romantic West'.

Louella Ballerino was the designer responsible for many of the Mexican-inspired clothes around in the 1940s. She used Mexican or Indian motifs in her cottons. She was one of the first American designers to use hand-blocked designs to give the fabric an original 'ethnic' look.

An exotic influence in sportswear came from Mexico, here demonstrated in a 1942 dress featured in the UK *Vogue* which was actually made, in the true spirit of make-do-and-mend, from three old dresses

Los Angeles designer Agnes Barrett came up with the amazing broomstick skirt. This was a cotton skirt wrapped around a broomstick while it was wet, then tied with string. It dried to produce an uneven crinkled effect. The skirt was sold with the broomstick, so when it was washed the customer could 'recrinkle' it. Sadly the broomstick skirt fell by the wayside under wartime restrictions.

Some things that were dropped during the war never really came back in fashion. Under British restrictions waistcoats used up valuable coupons, while the Americans banned them altogether. The conservative three-piece suit has never re-asserted itself over the more youthful two-piece. Due to a shortage of wool, socks with garters or suspenders disappeared. Short socks have remained in fashion ever since. The 1950s also saw a trend for tight sweaters that were short in the body. These began during the war due to the wool shortage.

One of the unforeseen consequences of the Utility and L-85 regulations is that consumers in Britain and America got used to a much higher quality of clothing. After the war, they were no longer content with shoddy goods. Clothes were built to last. Natural fibres were used – wool for winter, cotton and linen for summer. More latitude was allowed in the cotton prints though. Bold contrasting colours were used in splashy abstract designs. These were supposed to inspire optimism and, in Britain, world-famous artists such as Graham Sutherland and Paul Nash were employed by the Cotton Board to come up with cheerful designs – which were also exported to Latin American. Patriotic British and American designs, flags, anchors, military emblems – were all used. Red, white and blue were, of course, the favourite colours. And vigorous checks and polka dots were widespread, especially in the US. Again these vigorous patterns were supposed to inspire optimism.

Paris dancer Micheline Bernardini models the very first bikini

The Birth of the Bikini

In 1943, the US government calculated that 10 per cent of the fabric of a woman's swim-suit could be saved by baring the midriff – and the two-piece was born. Three years later, Louis Reard, a little known French designer, called his two piece design 'bikini' – after the American nuclear tests on Bikini Atoll. His designs were even more revealing than the wartime swimwear and his motivation was not a fabric shortage!

Precursor to the bikini was the two-piece hugely popular through the Forties; this fashionable outfit was in fact a 'three piece playsuit'

'The girl in the defense industry
She wears a coverall for work and
and nervous energy. And look at
out of the envelope each week!'

WOMAN AT WAR

really has all the luck.

hereby saves clothes, time, money,

all the nice green cash she picks

McCall's magazine 1942

Women of the ATS – the
Auxiliary Territorial
Service – servicing a
fighter plane during the
Battle of Britain

World War II was very much a woman's war. Not only did women man the factories, as they had in World War I, they also joined up. Women were recruited into the armed forces in Britain from 1938. At the height of the war, there were around half-a-million in the three women's services – the ATS, the WRNS and the WAAF.

The uniform of the Women's Auxiliary Territorial Service was modelled closely on that of the Women's Royal Naval Service. Initially, like those of the WRNS and the WAAF, it was blue because it would have been more difficult to find cosmetics to match a khaki outfit. This was not a trivial consideration. It was recognised from the beginning that the design and look of the uniform would have a critical effect on recruitment, morale and discipline.

However, on active service, women anti-aircraft gunnery teams wore men's battle dress. Ambulance drivers and other women in the auxiliary services abandoned uniform skirts for trousers.

Victorian starched nurses uniforms were found to be impractical in field hospitals. They were replaced by a new and simpler uniform designed by Norman Hartnell.

The Irish-born fashion designer Digby Morton designed a new uniform for the Women's Voluntary Service, who organised soup kitchens, food for the troops in transit and helped the people who had lost their homes in the blitz. The uniform was initially plain green. But this was considered to be an unlucky colour, so a dash of grey was added to the material.

Princess Elizabeth, the future Queen, changing a wheel as part of her officer training with the ATS

Complete with a stars-and-stripes head turban, a girl displays a 1945 'American Forces in London' scarf

Men in Uniform

American GIs stationed in Britain were warned: 'Remember how long the British alone have held Hitler off. If the British look dowdy and badly dressed it is not because they do not like good clothes or know how to wear them. All clothes are rationed. Old clothes are good form.' Meanwhile the British were told: 'Though we may be spiritually far more civilised, materially they have the advantage.' This was a genuine problem between the allies. Before seeing US uniforms few British soldiers realised how ill-designed and ill-fitting theirs was. Under wartime restrictions, pointed sleeve cuffs and pocket pleats were out and smart, ceremonial dress uniforms were dropped. Beside the Tommy, the GI looked like an officer. For both British and Americans, the elite were airmen, romantic figures after the Battle of Britain. In his book The Last Enemy, fighter pilot Richard Hillary compared modern-day airmen to medieval knights engaged in one-to-one combat with the foe. Airman wore sheepskin jackets, distinguishing them amongst servicemen, which the RAF called Irvins and the USAAF called Shearlings. Credit for the design goes to Anglo-American designer Charles James who had made a quilted ladies' jacket in Chinese silk before the war began.

Marlon Brando in his 1951

T-Shirt-stretching role in *A*

Streetcar Named Desire

The T-Shirt

The Pentagon had a clothing problem. After the Japanese attack on Pearl Harbour in 1941, eleven million American men were drafted, and uniforms had to be found for them all. Easy-to-manufacture, durable and all-purpose garments had to be designed. The US Navy solved one of its problems in 1942 with the development of the T-type shirt. This was a short-sleeved, round-necked garment in knitted cotton which would serve both as a shirt in the Pacific and an undershirt in colder climates.

At first it was produced only in white. But soon the habit of printing on the shirt – usually the name of a unit or military base – became popular. Because the T-shirt – as it became known – saw so much action during the Pacific war, it came to epitomise masculinity. Marlon Brando boosted its popularity by wearing a T-shirt in the movie *A Streetcar Named Desire* in 1951. And with *The Wild One* in 1953, the T-shirt became the full-blown icon of the counter-culture.

The bulk of British women were put to work in industry. At first, they were attracted by wages. But as early as 1941, the Ministry of Labour found that there was a labour shortage of two million workers. Conscription was introduced. Single women between eighteen and twenty-four were called up and 'mobile' married women – those who did not have commitments to keep them at home – were directed into work, often a long way from their homes. By 1943, 57 per cent of the workforce were women. Ninety per cent of all single women and 80 per cent of 'mobile' married women were working. But labour shortages persisted, so in April 1943, Minister of Labour Ernest Bevin decided to register 'immobile' women and raised the registration age to fifty-one – bringing along the charge that he was drafting 'grannies'.

However, hard work and short rations seems to have suited many of them.

'Englishwomen have never looked prettier than they do these days when they are dressing more simply, often going hatless, and working so hard that sleep comes easy at night, bombers or no bombers,' Mollie Panter-Downes wrote in her letter from London in the *New Yorker*.

After all, there were always ways to have fun. The story is told of one determined debutante, who had gone to work in an aircraft factory immediately after the outbreak of war. She would get off work, change into a long evening dress, dance the night away at the '400' Club, then be back at her lathe at eight o'clock the next morning.

In America too, women joined the armed services. This had distinct advantages for those who were fashion conscious. After years of dressing the Duchess of Windsor, Mainbocher designed the women's uniforms for the US Navy and the American Red Cross, while Philip Magnone came up with the women's uniforms for the US Army.

The munitions and aircraft factories were full of women production line workers – here seen polishing aircraft gun turrets

Like the corresponding men's uniforms, theirs were definately considerably more stylish than their British counterparts. They did at least fit.

In America, the labour shortage was not quite so acute as it was in Britain. Nevertheless, with huge numbers of men being drafted into the military, only women could make up the short-fall in the labour market and around one third of the female population did go to work. Overalls, dungarees and trousers became fashionable. At Sperry Gyroscope in the US, Vera Maxell was called into design the women's coveralls.

'The girl in the defense industry really has all the luck,' wrote *McCall's* magazine in 1942. 'She wears a coverall for work and thereby saves clothes, time, money, and nervous energy. And look at all the nice green cash she picks out of the envelope each week!'

The fashion for women in trousers really began in 1933, when Marlene Dietrich began wearing trouser suits as a practical working outfit on the film set. Other stars soon followed, but until the outbreak of war they were still considered avant garde, even by those women who were wearing beach pyjamas – the flapping bell-bottomed trousers and were worn over swim-suits.

But with the advent of war everyone copied Marlene Dietrich's grey flannel trousers. They were cut like a man's and opened at the side like a sailors.

Marlene Deitrich wearing
the grey flannel trousers
she made famous

Schiaparelli was also ahead of the game. In 1939, she had shown an 'alert' suit. This was a highly practical all-in-one trouser suit. It zipped up and was designed to be worn with damp-proof boots. The wearer could be ready for fight or flight within seconds. This was the forerunner of the one-piece zip-up siren suit which became popular as air-raid shelter wear during the blitz in London. Even Churchill wore one.

In London, where the threat of a gas attack was strongest, Harvey Nichols produced a hooded gas suit for women made of oiled silk. It was designed to be slipped over ordinary clothes in 35 seconds and the store promised that, in it, the wearer could safely cover a distance of two hundred yards through mustard gas. The outfit came in rose, pastel pink, apricot, eau-de-nil green and amethyst.

Women wore slacks for comfort, even pregnant. women. This was not uncommon in the war years. There was an average yearly increase in the birthrate of 29.6 per cent in the US during the decade and the Sears catalogue put on extra pages of maternity wear and baby clothes, filling the pages usually reserved for formal gowns. Weddings were popular too and jewellery vital. In 1944, Sears had an engagement ring with a price tag of $4,900.

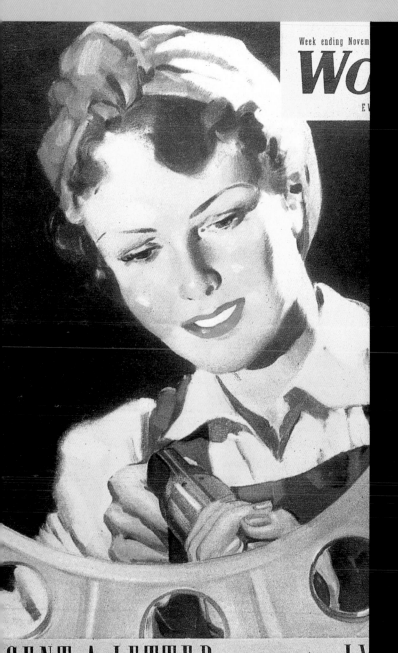

Week ending Novem

Wo
E
SENT A LETTER *story by* IV

Turbans and Snoods

Hats remained in vogue throughout the war. But in Britain and America, material rationing limited their size and flamboyancy. The only way to make them stylish was to wear them at an accentuated angle – tipped over the forehead to planted on the back of the head. Resourceful women also found they could enliven small Utility bonnets with flowers and ribbons. With women working more in factories, hats were increasingly replaced by head scarves and turbans – which had already come into fashion in the 1930s. Another variation was the snood. Snoods were either made from fabric or crocheted or knitted out of yarn and held the hair in place at the neck. Knitted or crochetted gloves were also run up by the resourceful.

Some smart ladies (left) were more prepared for air raids than others, chic in air raid suit and matching gas mask holder; the *Vogue* cartoon described the girls in Paris sheltering in the Ritz in 'satin pyjamas, hood coats . . . by Molyneaux and Piquet'

Lace blouses at 2,500 francs and pullovers at 3,000 francs

Despite Schiaparelli's idea of introducing huge pockets that would store everything a woman needed for the duration, the handbag remained a vital accessory. In fact, the modern shoulder bag with the owners initials on it dates from the war, when women got used to carrying gas mask holders slung over one shoulder.

Copious bags with shoulder straps were used for day-time wear. With evening wear, handle-less clutch bags were popular. And small box bags in patent leather with a make-up mirror in the lid were common.

Gloves too slowly went out of fashion during the war, especially among women used to getting their hands dirty in factories. But in the higher realms of society, suede gloves became fashionable. These were worn causally though. Elbow-length gloves were pushed down the arm – and 'crushed'. With evening wear, rayon jersey gloves, with elasticated threads, reached the height of fashion in 1944.

With the liberation of France, extravagant Paris fashions became the centre of controversy. The garments in the Paris collections had cuffed sleeves, superfluous buttons, pocket flaps, inessential pleats and loose Magyar sleeves – everything which was forbidden in the UK and US.

While clothing in Britain and the US remained strictly rationed, unrationed *haute couture* dresses contained acres of extraneous material in the sleeves and skirts. Silk stockings and fur coats were on sale in the shops around the Place de la Concorde. But the number of Parisian women who could afford them were tiny. Silk stockings

cost 700 francs. Even rayon ones, at 150 francs, were out of the reach of the ordinary Parisienne. Lace blouses at 2,500 francs and pullovers at 3,000 francs were on sale at a time when most women were wearing wooden-soled shoes and cardigans knitted out of string.

The US War Production Board censored any reference to Paris fashions in case they somehow incited American manufacturers to break the L-85 regulations. What made matters worse was that France was appealing for clothing at the same time. Although those who had done well out of the war could afford couture clothes, the poorest in society were even worse off than they had been under the Germans.

Ordinary Parisian women were now reduced to wearing anything they could get their hands on and the fuel shortage meant that they had to wear everything they had at the same time to keep warm. French women began to wear discarded men's trousers. Bright coloured patches and collars gave a new lease of life to old clothes. And in the absence of shoe leather, cork-soled wedges and joined wooden clogs had to do.

Molyneux and Schiaparelli returned to Paris and their collections in the autumn of 1945 showed a new sensitivity to the Allies sensibilities. The amount of material used in a dress was restricted to 3 meters (around 4 yards). But in January 1946, British *Vogue* pointed out that some Parisian dresses still contravened UK austerity regulations. They used buttons for ornamentation and wasted fabric on turn-back cuffs and pocket flaps.

Clothes were practical – left, from the Sears catalogue of Fall/Winter 1942-43 – as were hairstyles; top opposite,

Ingrid Bergman with the Marie Cut, considered even more practical than the Liberty, in *For Whom The Bell Tolls*

Hair

Hair styles had grown longer during the 1930s but, in wartime, women were urged to have their hair cut short in more practical styles. The Liberty Cut, which only needed trimming once a month, was popular, along with the Victory Roll and the close-cropped Vingle. In Britain, women had to wash their hair with home-made shampoo. One popular style was rolling the hair around a stuffed stocking to give it more bulk. Perms and peroxides were available and hairdressers remained open late, often after midnight for shift workers. British women had little money to spend. On the other hand, there was very little else to spend it on and a professional shampoo and set was a welcome luxury.

The Gas Mask Holder

Throughout Europe and even, briefly, in the US after Pearl Harbour, the gas mask became the vital accessory. Grim though the prospect of chemical warfare was, the gas mask holder became a popular fashion item. Elizabeth Arden designed a white velvet gas mask holder-cum-vanity case, while the hat-maker Aage Thaarup combineed a gas mask with a set of dice and a hip flask. The case was covered in poetry. These fashionable gas mask holders became the prototypes of the latterday shoulder bag.

HOORAY
HO

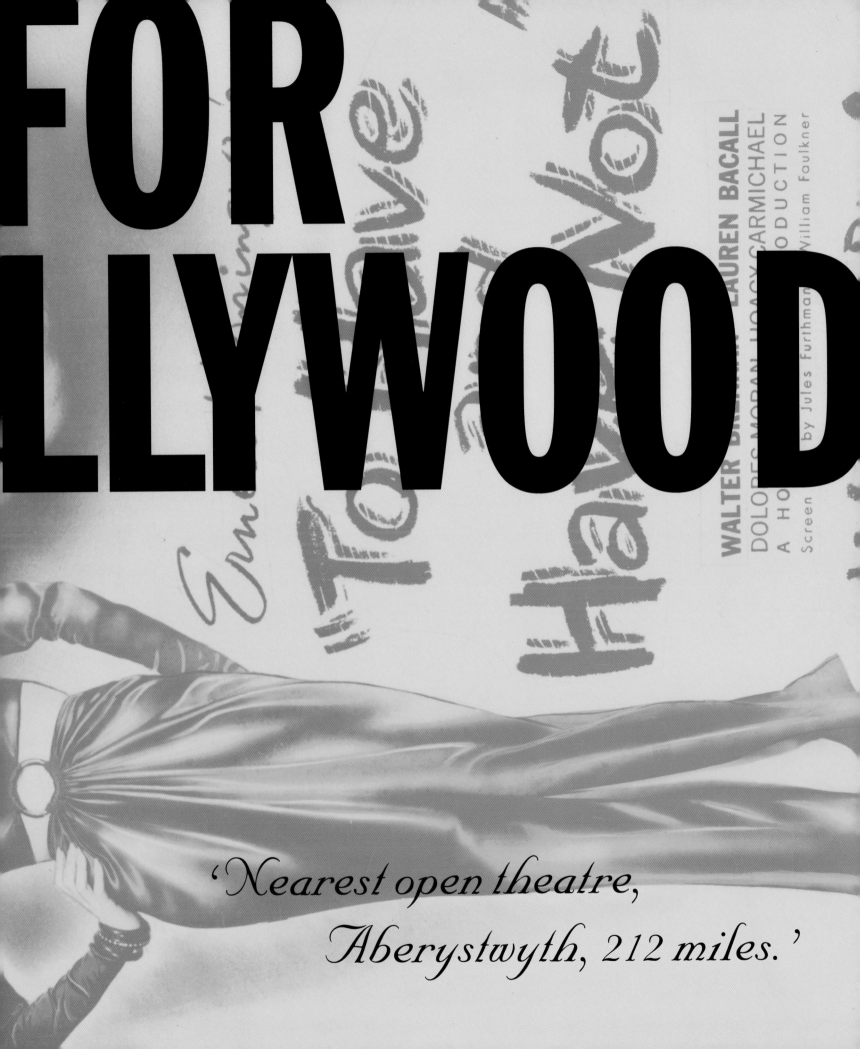

FOR
LLYWOOD

WALTER BR... LAUREN BACALL
DOLORES MORAN HOAGY CARMICHAEL
A HO...
Screen ...by Jules Furthman ...William Faulkner
...ODUCTION

'Nearest open theatre,
Aberystwyth, 212 miles.'

On both sides of the Atlantic, the cinema was mobilised in the war effort. It provided a vital channel of communication, with its newsreel, government information films, propaganda and morale-boosting movies.

Oddly, in Britain, the war began with the panic closing of all the cinemas and theatres in London and other major cities. One of the London theatres had put the jocular notice outside: 'Nearest open theatre, Aberystwyth, 212 miles.'

The reasoning behind the closing of the cinemas and theatres was that they were particularly vulnerable to bombing. But it was soon realised that keeping places of entertainment closed was bad for morale. So despite the risk involved, they were soon re-opened.

When the siren sounded, the projectionist would inform the audience with a slide. In a theatre, the manager would make an announcement from the stage. But then the show would continue as usual. Most people in the audience would stay put, even when the theatre was shaking from bombs being dropped nearby.

The first films to go on general release in the UK after the cinemas re-opened were *Jamaica Inn*, starring Charles Laughton, and *Goodbye, Mr Chips*, with Greer Garson and Robert Donat. Comedian Will Hay and ukulele-strumming George Formby did their best to keep morale up. Then came the American blockbusters *The Wizard of Oz* and *Gone With The Wind*. The scene when Scarlet O'Hara, played by English actress Vivien Leigh, has to make a dress out of old curtains in post-bellum Georgia struck a particular a chord with British audiences, who were soon to face similar hardships.

Even before America came into the war, the film industry was a great source of succour for the British. Hollywood was full of talented refugees

English rose Vivien Leigh as the fiery Scalet O'Hara in the American Civil War epic *Gone With The Wind*

who had fled Hitler's Germany and the occupied countries. It had long been home to a large colony of English actors and film-makers, and was also traditionally run by Jews whose sympathies were decidedly anti-Nazi. This all gave Hollywood a distinctly pro-British bent. But the moviemakers still had to be careful. The House Committee on Un-American Activities under Congressman Martin Dies Jr were examining the movie industry closely for political bias in a forerunner of the McCarthy witch-hunts of the 1950s. James Cagney, Humphrey Bogart, Fredric March and Francis Lederer were all reported to the Dies Committee as Communist sympathisers. All angrily denied it, but the accusations left an atmosphere of suspicion and mistrust. Anything too obviously pro-British, or anti-German, would have been investigated.

But one way around this was to go back to the English classics like *Jane Eyre* – which was made in 1934 and remade in 1943 – in order to stress the common heritage and common interests of all the English-speaking peoples. If that was too subtle, the studios could dress their political message up in lavish costume dramas. Just how far they could go was dictated by Roosevelt's speeches.

The bustles, wasp-waist and full skirts seen in these costume dramas were soon to be seen again Dior's New Look. Dior himself spent part of the war working on costume dramas for the French film industry.

After the bombing of Pearl Harbour everything changed. Gallant little Britain standing alone against the Nazi hordes became an essential strand of American propaganda. The distinctly pro-British tear-jerker *Mrs Miniver*, starring Greer Garson and Walter Pidgeon, came out in 1942. It showed the struggles and hardships of a plucky middle-class family in a country village in war-torn Britain. It

was not necessarily a picture of themselves that the British easily recognised, but it roused thousands of Americans to pack 'Bundles for Britain'. *Mrs Miniver* was also America's first chance to see the Utility clothes Brits were wearing – fashions that were soon to become their own under the Limiting Orders. The effect of the rose-covered hat worn by the eponymous Mrs Miniver was felt, not just in America, but also in Paris – where the style became the rage even though they had not seen the film.

Mrs Miniver was seen by one man in Germany though. It was studied by the Nazi propaganda minister Joseph Goebbels – not for its fashions but as a masterpiece of understated propaganda.

A poster for *Mrs.MInerva*, the American-made look at life in wartime Britain, that captivated the British, the Americans, the French and even Dr.Goebbels!

With record hits like 'Boogie Woogie Bugle Boy' and various film cameos, the Andrews Sisters – seen here in 'civvies' on a visit to London just after the War – epitomised the American girl-in-uniform

Without the counterbalance of Paris, Hollywood now ruled the world of fashion. In 1942, movie clothes designer Adrian moved into couture clothes. Another Hollywood designer, Irene, began producing ready-to-wear ranges for the Los Angeles store Bullock's Wiltshire. Robert Riley, head of the Fashion Institute of New York, praised them highly and Irene's clothes are still collectors items today.

But all was not plain sailing for Hollywood. Hundreds of the studio staff were drafted or moved into war work. There were a great many budget cut backs and, technically, the studios suffered exactly the same clothing restrictions as the rest of the civilian population.

But Washington was aware of the very real need for Hollywood glamour and its affect on morale, during the suffering of war.

Fred Astaire and Ginger Rogers simply could not be seen to make do and mend. In 1944 with the war at its height Ginger Rogers wore an outrageously expensive outfit made from sequins and ranch mink in the film *Lady in the Dark*. However, for *Meet Me in St Louis* which was made that same year, rayon had to be used instead of silk for almost every one of the costumes.

The shiny bugle beads that had given the 1930s' spectaculars glitz came from Czechoslovakia and their supply was cut off by Hitler. Satin, brocade, crêpe, and gold and silver lamé were all in short supply and wardrobe mistresses had to cannibalise old costumes to make new ones.

Marlene Dietrich's costume in *Flame of New Orleans* made a huge impact. But it was made in lace. This was 1941 and the L-85 order had banned its use, so no-one could copy it. But Deanne Durbin's white organdie dress in the 1941 movie *Nice Girl?* became the model for thousands of teenager girls' high-school prom dresses.

During the war Hollywood went in for a number of movies of pure entertainment and escapism. Bing Crosby, Bob Hope and Dorothy Lamour's 'Road' films began in 1940 with *Road to Singapore*. Two more 'Road' pictures were released by the end of the war. Betty Grable went *Down Argentina Way* and Deanna Durbin dressed to go on her *Spring Parade* in 1940. These movies all helped link exotic clothes with relentless optimism.

Sweater Girls

In America, one of the the defining fashion items of the
1940s was the sweater. Lana Turner, the original
'sweater girl', instigated the craze when she wore a tight,
figuring-hugging sweater in *They Won't Forget* (1937).
Ann Sheridan - Hollywood's 'oomph girl' and the most
outstanding of the sweater-girl faction at the time - was
actually called to intervene in an industrial dispute when
war production was curtailed at the Vought-Sikorsky
Aircraft Corporation in the 1940s after over fifty women
were sent home for wearing sweaters. The company first
insisted that the ban was on moral grounds, but when the
women's union pointed out that sweaters were permitted
inside the company's offices, they then claimed the ban
was on safety grounds. Sheridan pointed out that the
problem was not actually with the sweaters themselves,
but while a little girl in a big sweater might cause a
safety hazard, a big girl in a small sweater would most
certainly constitute a moral hazard.

Hair - Veronica Lake

Movie-star Veronica Lake was famous for her 'peekaboo'

hairstyle, with locks cascading over one eye. This was

thought to be dangerous for women working in factories.

Bending over machinery, the hair could easily get tangle

and she was persuaded to publicly change her style.

Instead, her hair was swept up, out of harms way.

Below, the 'Brazilian Bombshell' Carmen Miranda in typically restrained headgear

Below, the 'Brazilian Bombshell' Carmen Miranda in typically restrained headgear

Despite wartime regulations, Betty Grable did manage to hold on to her one-piece swim-suit and the shot with her looking over her shoulder became one of the GI's favourite pin ups. A twice-lifesize picture of her hung over the entrance of the Pavilion cinema in London's Piccadilly Circus.

Brazilian bombshell Carmen Miranda glamorised the turban, which factory girls used to keep their hair out of the machinery. Her wedge shoes too were copied, especially when shoe manufacturers turned over to cork and wooden-soled shoes.

However, the movie industry in both Britain and America was not the passive tool of government propaganda. In the UK, the Films Division of the Ministry of Information objected to Noël Coward's *In Which We Serve* in 1943. Although the film was based on a real incident, where Coward's friend Lord Louis Mountbatten had lost HMS *Kelly* to German torpedos off Crete, the Ministry thought it was defeatist to show a British ship being sunk. Luckily, Coward had friends in high places and the film was made. When it was shown in America, it was hailed as 'the first real great picture of World War II' - though the American censor had trouble

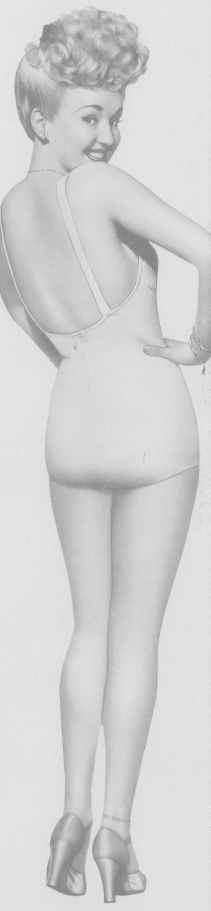

with it too. The Hays Office cut out the words 'God', 'hell', 'damn' and 'bastard'. Later, they allowed the 'bastard' back. After all, the film did depict men who were at war and therefore under a certain amount of stress.

Alfred Hitchcock committed the same folly in *Lifeboat* in 1944. This time a passenger ship was sunk by U-boats. But he filmed it in Hollywood, which experienced less government interference than Pinewood – perhaps because Hollywood is over two thousand miles from the seat of government. *Lifeboat* is most notable for Tallulah Bankhead, whose hairstyle and outfit are barely ruffled by the privations of an open boat.

Orson Welles' *Citizen Kane*, made in 1941, was hardly the greatest advertisement for American democracy. Nor did it show that America was always right to go to war. The film shows the newspaper magnate, a thinly disguised William Randolph Hearst, practically manufacturing the Spanish-American War of 1898. And *A Walk in the Sun* (1945) has been hailed as the greatest anti-war film of all time. The movie's message can hardly have been a surprise to the censor as it was made by

Lewis Milestone who had directed *All Quiet on the Western Front* fifteen years before.

Despite *Bataan*, *49th Parallel*, *We Dive at Dawn*, *The Way to the Stars* and *A Yank in the R.A.F*, which British audiences loved when it played in Britain in 1942, costume dramas depicting scenes from British history remained the staple diet of the war years. *The Young Mr Pitt* (1942) showed Britain standing alone and saving Europe. John Gielgud played Disraeli in *The Prime Minister* (1940), while Laurence Olivier played Nelson with Vivien Leigh in *That Hamilton Woman* (1941), released as *Lady Hamilton* in Britain. Churchill watched it often and cried during the scene where Nelson is killed at Trafalgar. But for women, these films were an opportunity to see clothes that were more sumptuous than anything they could dream of wearing in wartime.

The most extravagant costumes of all were the outfits worn in the wedding scene of Laurence Olivier's *Henry V* (1944). The effect was further heightened as the film was made in Technicolor. The story is, of course, about England going to war and, against the odds, winning.

The unlikely film to have the biggest fashion impact was *Casablanca* with Humphrey Bogart and Ingrid Bergman

But probably the most famous film made during World War II was *Casablanca* (1943). It showed off the new restricted American fashions and turned the trenchcoat – earlier a garment traditionally worn by mobsters – into something the good guy could wear. It could even be crumpled and you did not have to do up the belt, just tie it.

After the war, films like *Brief Encounter* (1945), *The Best Years of Our Lives* (1946) and *The Third Man* (1949) introduced the audience to the grim realities of the post-war world. Nevertheless *The Wicked Lady* (1945), which showed a splendid amount of cleavage, *Anna Karenina* (1948) with Vivien Leigh and even David Lean's *Great Expectations* (1946) and *Oliver Twist* (1947) reminded audiences that there was a time when women wore bustles and crinolines, corsets and acres and acres of material.

At the same time, something was happening to the female form, as portrayed by Hollywood. It began with *The Outlaw* in 1943. In the movie, the newcomer Jane Russell, is no flat-chested austerity girl in a L-85 suit. Producer-director Howard Hughes designed a wire-frame brassiere which cantilevered Russell's bosom to stunning effect while leaving her shoulders bare. Hughes was a very talented engineer – *The Outlaw* had been shot mainly at night because Hughes worked during the day designing aeroplanes for Henry Kaiser.

One man, Russell Birdwell, was hired specifically to publicise Jane Russell's breasts. But the campaign, which emphasised Russell's cleavage, fell foul of the Hays Office. A master of publicity, Hughes then held the movie back for three years, blaming the censors. When the film was eventually released, it caused a sensation. Hughes, it seems, had anticipated the returned of the rounded, full-figured women seen in the New Look by a full four years.

The shape of things to come

Hollywood seemed to anticipate Dior's New Look. For some years, they had promoted full-figured women. Jane Russell was followed by Frances Vorne, who was the 'pin-up girl of 1944'. She was known at 'the Shape'. Virginia Mayo was elected Stars and Stripes 'Miss Cheesecake 1948' and Ava Gardner eased out Lana Turner. Female movie stars were groomed by Anita Colby. A former model, she was known as 'the Face' and starred in the 1944 Cover Girl. Then she was a beauty consultant and was hired by David O. Selznick as 'charm' instructor to his female stars. In an attempt to compete with Hollywood, the British company Rank set up its 'Charm School'. One of its first graduates was fifteen-year-old Diana Dors, who had won her first bathing-beauty contest at the age of thirteen. She was labelled 'the sultry blonde bombshell with the wiggle' and was launched at the Venice Film Festival in a gondola wearing a diamond-studded mink bikini. But the brightest star at the close of the decade was Elizabeth Taylor. Although she was just seventeen in 1949, she was already voluptuous.

Jane Russell poses for the then-notorious portrait that featured on the publicity material for Howard Hughes' 1943 *The Outlaw*

ON CAMERA

Sumptibus Medii Templi extructa
An 168?

Gulielmo Whitelocke Arm Thesaur

Fashion photography changed radically with the coming of World War II. No longer could the doyens of *Vogue*, Cecil Beaton, Man Ray, Horst P. Horst, George Hoyningen-Huene and Edward Steichen, pose languid models seductively in well-lit Hollywood-inspired sets, often with their cigarette as an accessory. Falling bombs brought a new realism. Models had to look like they drove jeeps rather than were chauffeured around in limousines.

Beaton particularly fell foul of the new mood. The society photographer of the 1930s, he showed reckless insensitivity by simply posing well-dressed models in front of the bomb-damaged buildings he found around London. Many were offended by the way these pictures seemed to exploit the victims of blitz for aesthetic ends.

Nevertheless Beaton is a key figure in the 1940s, not least because so many of the newer generation of photographers who sprung up after the war found themselves reacting against him. Beaton had begun his interest in photography in 1921 when he watched his sister's nanny taking pictures with a Box Brownie. After that he built his own camera, a tiny device, and began experimenting. In 1926, he made his first contribution to *Vogue*, beginning an association between Beaton and *Vogue* lasting fifty years.

Beaton made a name for himself with a portrait of the Sitwells and a picture of the Duchess of Buccleuch, surrounded by roses and soap clouds. *Vogue*'s publisher Condé Nast was a fan. But when he watched Beaton at work, he insisted he change to a camera that used large 10 x 8 inch plates. This produced the flat effect in Beaton's later work.

In the 1930s, Beaton was strongly influenced by Surrealism. At that time, the Surrealist artist Man Ray worked for *Vogue* as a fashion photographer. What Beaton picked up on particularly was the artificiality created by Surrealism which, he thought, perfectly suited fashion photography.

Cecil Beaton's famous portrait of the Sitwells (top to bottom Osbert, Edith and Sacheverell), heavily influenced by the Surrealists

Opposite, the memorable Beaton photograph from UK *Vogue* in September 1941, featuring a model in a suit by Digby Morton

Previous page, model Jean Patchett in Edwin Blumenfeld's 1950 *Vogue* cover 'Doe Eye'

Beaton would build sets in the studio to use as a backdrop, almost as if he was photographing a movie still. But when the war came, this was no longer possible and he began shooting in the street.

Half-Estonian, half-American, Baron George Hoyningen-Huené was another leading fashion photographer at the beginning of the 1940s. He had started as an assistant to a *Vogue* staff photographer in Paris in 1923. One day the staff photographer failed to turn up to a shoot. Hoyningen-Huené called the magazine's offices to tell them. The elaborate studio set had been built. The models had arrived and he was told to shoot the pictures himself. He did.

Fortunately, Hoyningen-Huené was not only a competent photographer, but he also had a great encyclopaedic knowledge of the new developing artistic movements – Dada, Surrealism, Cubism, Expressionism, Futurism – that were slogging it out in Paris at the time. On the strength of that first shoot, he became *Vogue*'s chief photographer.

His work was known for its static poses. At that time, shooting quality fashion photographs outdoors in natural light was not practical. So bathing suits and ski-wear had to be shot in the studio. Nevertheless Hoyningen-Huené managed to capture the feeling of the outdoors in these studio shots. But he is perhaps better known for his shots of models in statuesque poses, or frozen as if in a classical frieze.

He was a great stylist and he would deliberately parody the work of other photographers just to show how easily he could plunder their trade secrets. He was also a great fan of Man Ray and introduced him to Mainbocher, who was working at *Vogue* at the time.

Hoyningen-Huené also brought one of the other great fashion photographers of the 1930s and 1940s to *Vogue*, Horst P. Horst. A student under the revolutionary architect Le Corbusier, Horst had

never taken a photograph in his life when the *Vogue*'s art director Dr Mehemed Fehmy Agha told him he could use the *Vogue* studios twice a week for two hours. His work overflowed with colour, but he maintained a solid, posed almost architectural feel that was ubiquitous in the 1930s.

Beaton, Hoyningen-Huené and Horst travelled between Paris, London and New York, working for all three editions of *Vogue*. They all specialised in posed studio work. In 1935, Leica developed a new camera with a shutter-speed of 1/1000 second. This allowed fashion photography out on the streets. One of the first to exploit this facility was Hungarian-born news photographer Martin Munkacsi. He photographed clothes in the real-life situations where they would actually be worn. Meanwhile Edward Steichen found a way to synchronise a 1/1000-second shutter speed to flash bulbs. This resulted in a colour spread capturing the action at the Radio City Music Hall.

With the war, things began changing at *Vogue*. The French edition was closed. And in 1941, Russian émigré Alexander Liberman, who had been editorial director of the influential magazine *Vu* in Paris, joined the staff of American *Vogue*. *Vu* was primarily a news magazine and Liberman imported some of the unposed realism of photojournalism into fashion photography.

'I was reacting against the pre-war pictures of Beaton and Horst, which seem like completely mannered exercises,' he said.

He immediately employed Erwin Blumenfeld who had been introduced to the editor of French *Vogue* Michel de Brunhoff by Cecil Beaton in Paris just before the war. Blumenfeld began working for *Vogue* there. A well-known early image was of famous model Lisa Fonssagrives – who later married fashion photographer Irving Penn – tottering on the topmost strut of the Eiffel Tower.

**The highly influential photograph by Surrealist Man Ray,
'Le Violin d'Ingres'**

Man Ray

Born Enamel Rabinovitch in Philadelphia 1890, he was a painter, yet his photography was highly influential in the 1930s and 1940s. In 1915, he and French Dadaist Marcel Duchamp formed a New York Dada group. He moved to Paris in 1921 and became involved in the Surrealist movement, but struggling to sell his work he took up photography, rediscovering cameraless photography, where objects are exposed directly on the photographic plate - he called them Rayographs, and he also experimented with solarisation. His experimental work was highly influential and Vogue invited him to provide fashion photography, for the inaugural issue of the French edition in August 1925. Fashion photographers, like Cecil Beaton, George Hoyningen-Huené and Horst P. Horst, featured Surrealist props, such as broken columns, in their photographs, but Man Ray eschewed these tricks. He used plain backdrops and depended on light and movement for effects. Instead of using static poses, he shot his sessions like a movie-director. When the Germans attacked Paris in 1940, Ray escaped to Los Angeles, returning to France in 1946. Later, he returned to painting, leaving photography behind him.

Blumenfeld was one of the first photographers to use a Hasselblad. It had a wide angle lens, giving pictures a new perspective. He also played with the raw image, in one of his classic shots he doctored a picture of a woman's face so that only one eye, the lips and a single beauty spot remained.

At American *Vogue*, Liberman employed younger photographers, including the talented Irving Penn, who had studied at the Pennsylvania Museum School of Industrial Art under Alexey Brodovitch, another influential figure of the day.

Brodovitch was a white Russian who fled to Paris in 1920 where he painted stage sets designed by Matisse and Picasso for the Diaghilev's Ballets Russe. Then he began designing the two influential art magazines *Arts et Métiers Graphiques* and *Cahiers d'Art*. He also won five medals for design at the Paris Exposition des Arts Décoratifs et Industriels Modernes, 1925. In 1930, he moved to the US where he set up the Pennsylvania Museum School of Industrial Art. In 1932, Carmel Snow took over *Harper's Bazaar*; he hired Brodovitch as art director. They ran the magazine for 24 years.

Brodovitch inspired young photographers such as Penn, who worked as an assistant to Brodovitch at *Harper's*. *Harper's* published some of his early work. Penn also worked with Brodovitch when he was employed as a design consultant to Saks Fifth Avenue, taking over the job when Brodovitch quit.

In 1942, Penn went to Mexico to paint. When he realised that he would never be better than mediocre as a painter, he returned to New York where he became Liberman's assistant on *Vogue*.

When Condé Nast died in 1942, his preference for the 10 x 8-inch plate camera died with him and Liberman was free to indulge his preference for a freer, more realistic style. He took on two more Russian émigrés, Constantin Joffé and Serge Balkin, who used Rolleiflexes. He also took on the 24-year-old American Frances McLaughlin who, he said, was free of the 'artificial grammar inherited from the European photographers'.

Liberman himself pursued as a photographer and sculptor outside his work at *Vogue*. He also acted as a tutor to young photographers he took on. He always showed the new recruits two photographs. One was Edward Steichen's portrait of Marion Morehouse wearing a dress by Cheruit taken in 1927. Although it is a straightforward posed shot, it puts Morehouse and the dress in their natural context. The other was a picture taken by Walker Evans in 1932, showing an elegant black man in a white suit at a newsstand in downtown Havana. It is a naturalistic shot but perfectly concentrates the viewers attention on the man's outfit.

As Liberman's assistant, Penn was asked to get photographers to find cover ideas. But he found it hard to tell experienced photographers like Blumenfeld and Horst what to do. Liberman then suggested Penn photograph the covers himself.

Penn brought to fashion photos a knowledge of classical art. His pictures were composed around sketches he and Liberman worked on. The results though posed, had none of the stagy quality that characterised Beaton's work.

At the same time as Irving Penn was rising to prominence, Brodovitch was encouraging young American photographer, Richard Avedon. Avedon turned up a *Harper's* offices carrying a portfolio of men in action he had taken. Brodovitch liked his work, particularly his use of focus – Avedon would blur parts of the picture to concentrate the eye.

Brodovitch commissioned Avedon, but his early work was disappointing as he was uneasy using professional models. Avedon asked editor Diana Vreeland to let him use his wife instead. They went on a location trip to Mexico, but a twelve-page feature Brodovitch cut to just two pages.

Opposite, model Lisa Fonssagrives poses on the Eiffel Tower in a shot by Erwin Blumenfeld, dress by Lucien Lelong, from French *Vogue* May 1939

A noted Norman Parkinson picture of 1937 from the pages of *Harper's Bazaar*

In 1945, Brodovitch gave Avedon a last chance, Avedon justified his faith and took shots showing a playful, touching freshness. Brodovitch was delighted but Vreeland was appalled. Avedon's models wore neither shoes nor gloves. She saw this as alien to *Vogue* philosophy and demanded to use Hoyningen-Huené. But he was by now tired of fashion and quit. In command Brodovitch and Avedon began stripping away the old sets. Between them, Penn, Avedon, Brodovitch and Landshoff freed fashion photography from the sharp focus of Beaton, Horst and Hoyningen-Huené, and breathed new fluid pulsating life into it.

Another rising star of the 1940s was Norman Parkinson. A Briton, he divided his life between fashion photography and farming. His women were idealised, gentle creatures often posed in green fields, very different from the harder, more street-wise girls that other American photographers had begun to use. Parkinson began working for *Vogue* in 1948. His celebration of nature can been seen to be harking back to a romanticised view of rural England. His view held sway, in Britain, at least, until a brasher new generation of young working class fashion photographers turned the world upside down in the 1960s.

The Models

Until the 1940s, models were called mannequins and were largely anonymous. But after the war they began to become famous in their own right. Their names, the diets and who they were going out with became international news.

One of the most famous English models was Barbara Goalen who first appeared in *Vogue* and *Harper's Bazaar* in 1947. Rationing had slimmed British women down. Goalen was what was just 7 stone (105 pounds), 33-18-31 and she had huge doeish eyes. She was a young widow with two small children, whom she supported by modelling. She got five guineas (£5.25) for an hour.

'Betina' worked at Jacques Fath and achieved notoriety modelling Rita Hayworth's wedding dress, when the film star was to marry Aly Khan. Another Fath model, 'Sophie', married Hollywood film director Anatole Litvak.

Jean Dawnay, a blonde ex-air hostess and daughter of the general, modelled for Dior for six months. This was a rare privilege for an English girl.

A true supermodel of her day, the elegant Barbara Goelen as she appeared in *Harper's*, April 1952

THE ASHES

Previous page: Left, a stone mason repairs blitz damage with an untouched St. Paul's Cathedral in the background. Right, the tiny mannequins on show in the Théâtre de la Mode

Australian soldiers and an airman celebrate VE Day, May 8th 1945, with some local London girls

THE RETURNING GI ALTHOUGH GI'S RETURNING HOME TO THE US KNEW FEWER RESTRICTIONS THAN THEIR BRITISH COUNTERPARTS, FEW HAD THE MONEY TO SPLASH OUT OF THE SEVEN ESSENTIAL OUTFITS FOR THE RETURNING SOLDIER OUTLINED BY THE *NEW YORKER* MAGAZINE. NEVERTHELESS, EX-SERVICEMEN RETURNING THE CIVILIAN LIFE WANTED A NEW LOOK. TIRED OF THEIR TIGHTLY TAILORED UNIFORMS, THEY FAVOURED BROAD-SHOULDERED DRAPE SUITS WITH ACRES OF FABRIC IN THE JACKET. CUFFS RETURNED TO TROUSERS AND THE POST-WAR STYLES SPORTED GENEROUS PLEATS AND PATCH POCKETS. 'LOAFER' JACKETS AND SPORTS COATS BECAME FASHIONABLE. AND BOYS' KNICKERBOCKERS EVENTUALLY WENT OUT AND SONS WERE DRESSED LIKE SMALLER VERSIONS OF THEIR FATHERS. WESTERN-STYLE RANCH CLOTHING AND CALIFORNIA BEACHWEAR WENT FROM STRENGTH TO STRENGTH AND DENIM RECEIVED A NEW BOOST BY A SPATE OF COWBOY FILMS. ROY ROGERS JEANS AND JACKETS APPEARED IN THE SEARS CATALOGUE, ALONG WITH SUSPENDER DUNGAREES FOR TODDLERS AND ROLLED-UP PEDDLE PUSHERS FOR TEENAGERS.

US clothing restrictions were lifted on VE-day – 8 May 1945 – though the price freeze imposed two years before remained in place until 1946. Clothing was soon plentiful again – it was easy for American munitions factories to turn their output back into civilian production. But in Europe, this took much longer. Many factories had been destroyed during the war. Docks and railways had also been targeted. Britain and the other European countries had been virtually bankrupted by the war effort.

After liberation, Paris was determined to put itself back at the heart of the fashion world. Within weeks Maggy Rouff, Lelong and Schiaparelli were showing 'liberation fashions'. Lelong celebrated with military accessories, such as a charm bracelet of tiny jeeps. Schiaparelli designed a dress with a bustle in the front. And Madame Lanvin appeared to let freedom go to her head with a backless and almost frontless evening gown called, appropriately, Liberty and a tiny pink frock called Free France. Prices were high, materials inferior and sales quite disappointing – but this may have been because many of the couturiers' best customers were in jail for supporting the Vichy government.

DUFFLE COATS AND REEFER JACKETS

Originally manufactured in Duffle in Belgium, these thick woolen coats were perfect for the often Artic conditions on the decks of the Royal Navy escorts to the North Atlantic convoys. Freezing temperatures also meant that fingers were too cold to deal with normal buttons and hence the familiar wooden toggles and loops were introduced. There was an army issue too and General Montgomery was seen wearing a duffle coat during the Normandy campaign and during the Battle of the Bulge.

After the war, a large number of these coats turned up in army surplus stores and were grabbed by students. And by the mid-1950s, the Duffle coat had lost the heroic aura of the North Atlantic and become the essential outfit for the Beatnik.

The American equivalent was the 'reefer' jacket, which was shorter but made out of similar thick woollen material. Reefer jackets, too, became the fashion among the young in the late 1950s and early 1960s.

Pierre Balmain's 'coolie coat' based on a worker's blouse, from a 1945 *Vogue*, photographed by Cecil Beaton

Above, back to civvy
street: men recently
discharged from the
Royal Air Force in
1945 visit an RAF
Civilian Clothing
Centre and exchange
their uniforms for the
civilian 'demob' (for
demobilisation) suits

THE DEMOB SUIT ON LEAVING THE ARMED FORCES, EVERY BRITISH

SERVICEMAN WAS GIVEN A SUIT – A TWO-PIECE, TO BE WORN WITH A PULLOVER RATHER THAN A

WAISTCOAT – A SHIRT, TWO COLLARS, A TIE, ONE PAIR OF CUFF-LINKS, TWO PAIRS OF SOCKS, A

HAT AND A PAIR OF SHOES. THE DEMOB SUIT WAS USUALLY A LIGHT COLOUR BECAUSE OF

SHORTAGE OF DYES. IT WAS DISTINGUISHED BY HAVING TWO BUTTON-HOLES – ONE IN EACH LAPEL – AND SOON BECAME SOMETHING OF A JOKE. LIKE BRITISH UNIFORMS, THEY WERE ALSO ILL-FITTING AND HOPELESSLY OUT OF DATE. SOME BLAMED THE TAILORS, SAYING AFTER SIX YEARS OF WAR, ALL THEY COULD COME UP WITH WAS A 1930S DESIGN. BUT GENERAL FEELING WAS THAT A CONSERVATIVE LOOK MET THE NEEDS OF THE TIMES. PEOPLE WANTED NOTHING MORE THAN FOR THE WORLD TO RETURN TO HOW IT HAD BEEN BEFORE THE CONFLAGRATION HAD STARTED. BESIDES, THE SMARTER, MORE FLASHY MODES OF DRESS HAD BEEN USURPED BY THE SPIVS AND RACKETEERS. NO-ONE TRUSTED FLAMBOYANCE.

MANY SERVICE GREATCOATS WERE STRIPPED OF THEIR INSIGNIA AND CONVERTED FOR CIVILIAN USE. IT WAS *DE RIGEUR* TO HAVE PIP-HOLES IN THE EPAULETTES OF THE COAT TO SHOW THAT YOU HAD BEEN AN OFFICER.

WHEN RATIONING ENDED, MEN WHO WERE GETTING THEMSELVES BACK ON THEIR FEET AGAIN CELEBRATED WITH THE BROAD DOUBLE-BREASTED SUITS THAT HAD BEEN POPULAR BEFORE THE WAR. TROUSERS BECAME FULLER AND COATS HAD WIDE V-SHAPED LAPELS.

THIS WAS NOT A STYLE THAT APPEALED TO ROYALTY AND JOHN TAYLOR, THE EDITOR OF THE *TAILOR AND CUTTER*, LAMBASTED THE DUKE OF EDINBURGH FOR FAILING TO PROVIDE THE FASHION LEAD THAT THE PRINCE OF WALES HAD PROVIDED BEFORE THE WAR. THE DUKE, HE SAID, LACKED FLAIR AND ORIGINALITY. HE DID NOT HAVE HIS TROUSERS PRESSED OFTEN ENOUGH. HIS POCKETS WERE STUFFED AND HE WENT BAREHEADED AT A TIME WHEN THE MEN'S HAT TRADE WERE PUSHING THE SLOGAN: 'IF YOU WANT TO GET AHEAD, GET A HAT.'

Auto tube news: Butyl increases wear, seals air

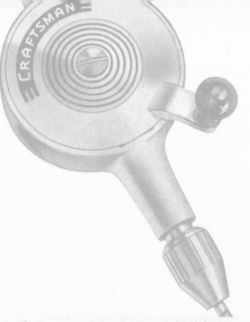

The news in tools: improved, streamlined designs

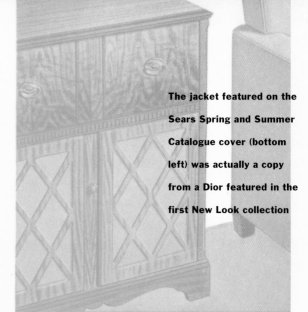

Radio news: less height, new beauty

The jacket featured on the Sears Spring and Summer Catalogue cover (bottom left) was actually a copy from a Dior featured in the first New Look collection

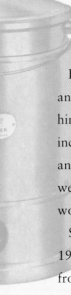

Health news: a home pasteurizer for safe milk

Style news for boys: smart plaid tee shirts

In 1944, Pierre Balmain decided to quit Lelong and go it alone, and Cecil Beaton was soon hailing him as the new rising star of fashion. He clients including Princess Radziwill, the Duchess of Kent and the Duchess of Windsor. His early innovations were low, square necklines and blouses based on workers' tops.

Skirts were already getting longer. In autumn 1945, Balenciaga was showing hemlines 15 inches from the ground. In New York in June 1946, American designers dropped hems three inches below the knee – which was 14 or 15 inches above the sidewalk. Some showed flared skirts and uneven handkerchief hems. Waistlines shrank, while gathers and big pockets emphasised rounded hips. In Britain to, even before the end of rationing, smart girls were letting their hems down.

The shape was changing too. In March 1946, the London collections showed rounded shoulders, after years of square ones. Molyneux exhibited a checked dress with padded hips – the shoulders were still square. *Harper's Bazaar* commented: 'Softer, rounder runs the London line. You have

hips. You have a waist. You have a bosom. You have round, natural shoulders.'

Harper's also reported from Paris that year: 'Skirts are definitely longer, averaging three to five inches below the knee.'

The hour-glass figure returned. Balenciaga now introduced suits with wasp waist, long jackets and padding over the hips. That year, most of the houses incorporated the narrow waist pioneered by Chanel and Lelong in 1939. Magyar sleeves and sloping shoulders appeared on coats and it was plain that a major new silhouette was emerging. No-one was quite sure what it was yet, but after years of a stern masculine look, things were now beginning to change. British *Vogue* of October 1946 greeted Paris's autumn collections with the headline: 'Paris revels in femininity.'

That same year, the strapless bra was invented. Silk was back in fashion for underwear, but not for hosiery. Improvements in the production of nylon meant it could be woven to make sheer, and seamless stockings. This advance spawned the new 'nude leg' look.

In 1947, Sears brought out their biggest spring catalogue for 25 years. Outer wear had soft curves, fullness and flare. The catalogue copy said: 'The new look is a long look. Skirts are longer. Waistlines are longer. Fabrics are used lavishly.' Everyone seemed to be groping towards a newer fashion, after the restrictions of war.

The first to spot where it would come from were Czech textile designers Lida and Zika Ascher, who had spent the war in London, where Molyneux had used their abstract patterns for his summer frocks. In 1946, they were in Paris to see the collections. At Lelong's, they saw one of Christian Dior's designs with sloping shoulders. This design looked so unique that Lida Ascher bought one in black. At the fitting she had some qualms, but it was too late to cancel the order.

She wore the dress next time they visited Pierre Balmain, who had been buying the Aschers' printed silk since he had left Lelong to set up on his own in 1944. Balmain took one look at the dress and said: '*Oh, c'est raté.* [That is a failure.] Leave it with me and I will improved it.'

He added a lot of coloured drapery around the waist. Lida, later, greatly regretted that she had had it altered.

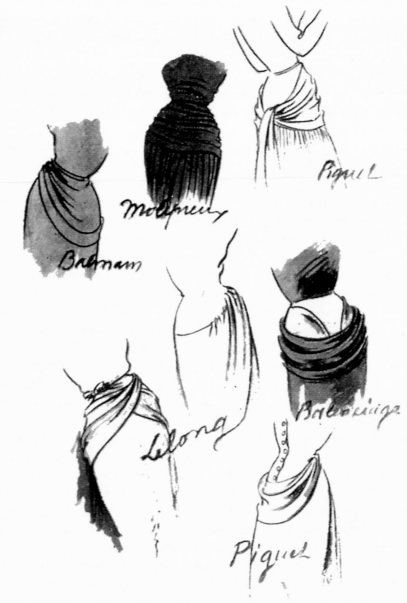

The Paris collections were dissected in detail in the January 1946 issue of *Vogue* (above) designers included Molyneaux, Balmain and Balenciaga; elsewhere (left) Paris designers like Lucien Lelong and Schiaparelli were seen to contravene UK utility regulations

THÉÂTRE DE LA MODE

AFTER FOUR YEARS OF THEIR OWN WAY, MANY BRITISH AND AMERICAN DESIGNERS BELIEVED FRENCH *HAUTE COUTURE* WAS DEAD. BUT THE FRENCH FASHION INDUSTRY SURVIVED THE WAR INTACT AND WANTED TO SHOW THAT IT WAS STILL ALIVE AND KICKING. OPPORTUNITY CAME IN 1944 WHEN RAOUL DAUTRY, HEAD OF ENTR'AIDE FRANÇAISE, AN ORGANISATION CO-ORDINATING THE FRENCH CHARITIES, SUGGESTED THE COUTURIERS STAGE A FUND-RAISING EXHIBITION. ROBERT RICCI, HEAD OF CHAMBRE SYNDICALE DE LA COUTURE PARISIENNE AND SON OF DESIGNER NINA RICCI, RECOGNISED THE EXHIBITION'S POTENTIAL. HE PLANNED TO SHOW THE FIRST POST-WAR PARISIAN COLLECTION, SPRING AND SUMMER 1945, IN MINIATURE ON SOME 200 TWO FEET TALL MANNEQUINS. THE EXHIBITION COULD TRAVEL AND SHOW THE WORLD, PARIS WAS BACK IN BUSINESS. IT WOULD BE CALLED THE THÉÂTRE DE LA

The obvious influence of the work of the Surrealists, Jean Cocteu and Picasso was evident in the mythical Centaurs and other fabled creatures in the Théâtre de la Mode tableaux

MODE. THE DOLLS WERE DESIGNED BY ELIANE BONABEL AND MADE BY ARTIST JEAN SAINT-MARTIN, (OF WIRE AND RESEBLING MODERN SCULPTURE), SCULPTOR JOAN REBULL MADE THE PLASTER HEADS. CHRISTIAN BÉRARD WAS ARTIST DIRECTOR OF THE PROJECT AND COMMISSIONED THE ARTIST ELITE OF PARIS – INCLUDING JEAN COCTEAU – FOR BACK DROPS. THEY GAVE

THEIR SERVICES FREE. THERE WAS A FUEL SHORTAGE AND SEAMSTRESSES, COBBLERS, MILLINERS AND GLOVEMAKERS

WORKED BY CANDLE-LIGHT IN FREEZING STUDIOS. INTENSE RIVALRY BETWEEN THE HOUSES MEANT THAT THEY WENT TO

EXTRAORDINARY LENGTHS TO UPSTAGE EACH OTHER. THE STRIPED FABRIC OF A CARVEN DRESS WAS CUT AND SEWN BACK

FOR SMALLER STRIPES. MATERIAL FOR PATOU WAS ESPECIALLY WOVEN SO THE FOLDS WOULD HANG PROPERLY. SILK UNDERWEAR WAS MADE AND MINIATURE JEWELLERY CAME FROM CARTIER AND VAN CLEEF & ARPELS. THE THÉÂTRE DE LA MODE OPENED IN THE LOUVRE ON 27 MARCH 1945. FOR THE IMPORTANT EVENT, THE GARDE RÉPUBLICAINE FORMED A GUARD OF HONOUR FOR OPENING NIGHT. OVER 100,000 PEOPLE SAW THE EXHIBITION IN PARIS. FEW COULD AFFORD ANYTHING, BUT THE COLOUR AND LUXURY OF THE THÉÂTRE DE LA MODE WAS PERFECT FOR POST-WAR PARIS. IT

Above, theatre within a theatre, as the mannequins face framed counterparts Left, a figure displaying a robe by designer Marcelle Alix when the Théâtre de la Mode toured in 1946

TRAVELLED AROUND THE EUROPEAN CAPITALS, AND TO NEW YORK. IN ALL THE EXCITEMENT ONE THING WAS OVERLOOKED.

CHRISTIAN DIOR, WORKING FOR LUCIEN LELONG, SUPPLIED TWO DRESSES. IN CONTRAST TO THE OTHER OUTFITS THEY HAD

NIPPED-IN WAISTS AND FULL SKIRTS – THE KEY FEATURES OF THE COMING NEW LOOK.

THE NE

'ARROGANTLY SWINGING THE

EIGHTY YARDS OF FABRIC),

TIGHT BODICES, THE WASP

BOUND ON BY VEILS UNDER

ON, CONTEMPTUOUSLY BO

STANDS LIKE NINEPINS....

SOUNDNESS WAS POSITIVELY

W LOOK

AND ITS IMPACT

ER WAST   ONE HAD

THE SOF

-WAISTS.   NY HATS

THE CHI   SWIRLED

WLING   SHTRAY

THIS NEW   SOFTNESS AND

VOLUPTUOUS.

ON 12 FEBRUARY 1947, WHEN THE EDITOR OF

HARPER'S BAZAAR, CARMEL SNOW, SAT DOWN

AT DIOR'S FIRST SHOW, SHE WAS HEARD

TO HISS CROSSLY: 'THIS HAD BETTER

BE GOOD.' THE WHOLE OF PARIS

WAS SHIVERING. COAL WAS IN

SHORT SUPPLY AND THE

TEMPERATURE FELL TO THIRTEEN

DEGREES BELOW FREEZING. IT WAS COLD IN

DIOR'S SALON IN THE AVENUE MONTAIGNE. BUT IT

WAS NOT ONLY THE CHILL THAT GAVE THOSE ASSEMBLED

GOOSEPIMPLES. IT WAS ALSO AN EXCITING, UNFAMILIAR SOUND – IT WAS

THE SWISH OF VAST PETTICOATS. THE MODELS STRODE IN, ERNESTINE CARTER

REPORTED IN BRITISH *HARPER'S BAZAAR*, 'ARROGANTLY SWINGING THEIR VAST

SKIRTS , THE SOFT SHOULDERS, THE TIGHT BODICES, THE WASP-WAISTS, THE TINY HATS

BOUND ON BY VEILS UNDER THE CHIN. THEY SWIRLED ON, CONTEMPTUOUSLY BOWLING OVER

THE ASHTRAY STANDS LIKE NINEPINS. THIS NEW SOFTNESS AND SOUNDNESS WAS POSITIVELY

VOLUPTUOUS.' CHEERS BROKE OUT AND SOME OF THE AUDIENCE WEPT. JANET IRONSIDE, WHO LATER

BECAME PROFESSOR OF FASHION DESIGN AT LONDON'S ROYAL COLLEGE OF ART, SAID THAT: 'IT WAS

LIKE A NEW LOVE AFFAIR, THE FIRST SIGHT OF VENICE, A NEW CHANCE, IN FACT A NEW LOOK AT LIFE.'

COR

The New Look needed
new support – literally; this
Dior foundation for the
1947 Paris collection was
described in *Vogue* as 'a
taffeta underbodice with
rose-ruffles at the breasts
and a ruffled hip…'

This foundation garment designed for the 1948 New Look collections made use of pads on the hips and shoulders in order to emphasise the tiny waist

The New Look was not the instant success that most people now believe it to have been. The French newspapers were on strike at the time, so few people knew about it. And most of the American buyers had already left town after snapping up all they wanted from the collections of designers like Lelong, Balmain, Rochas, Piguet, Fath and Balenciaga.

'Poor things,' said Carmel Snow, after the show, 'they will have to come back.'

Dior had called his first collection *Corolla* – the whorl of a leaf or petal before it opened out. He wanted his dresses and his models to look like flowers – bright, cheerful, natural. The *Corolla* was also said to be a dancing line. The petticoats, the narrow waistline and moulded bust with irregular pleats, *Elle* said, all were suggestive of dance.

At the *Corolla*, Dior also introduced the *Figure of Eight* line – eight, Dior believed, to be his lucky number. The *Figure of Eight* took the same silhouette even further with the bust underlined, the waist narrowed and the hips accentuated.

After the show, Carmel Snow remarked to Dior: 'It's quite a revolution, dear Christian. Your dresses have such a new look.'

In 1947, few people outside the Parisian couture houses knew who Dior was. The newsagencies spelt his name 'Diaure' or 'd'Yorre'. But *Life* magazine picked up on those two words – 'New Look'.

It was not until Dior's second collection that the name 'New Look' really stuck. Soon even the French were calling it 'le New Look'. But even in February 1947, it was clear that something was going on. *Harper's* ran the headline: 'Paris Rounds Every Line.' Even the models acted differently, *Harper's* noted: 'The stance is a hippy one... a new way of walking.' What's more, the price tags were terrifying – up to £250 per garment.

There was nothing very new about the 'New Look'. Dior's hemlines were not any longer than those Balenciaga had unveiled the year before, though his skirts were voluminous. Dior insisted that his designs were not revolutionary, but only conservative. They harked back to the styles of the *Belle Époque*, the secure and comfortable period before World War I when Dior had grown up.

'We were emerging from the period of war, of uniforms, of women-soldiers built like boxers,' Dior said. 'I drew women-flowers, soft shoulders, fine waists like liana and wide skirts like corolla.'

Above, drawings by the illustrator SAM from the 1947 Dior collection

The impact of the New Look was unprecedented. In the midst of the austerity and hardship that most people in Europe were still suffering, here was great opulence. Americans saw it as nothing short of a scandal. How could a Frenchman be so unpatriotic as to squander huge amounts of material when his country was nearly bankrupt? A Dior skirt took over 25 yards of fabric to make.

However, this sudden riot of extravagance served, happily, to remind the people that the horrific suffering and torment of World War II was now

Dior's taffeta dinner dress (right) was made from 25 yards of material. 'Your own shoulders' said *Vogue* 'plus padded hips'

finally over. The world was now truly at peace and good times were just around the corner.

Harper's Bazaar said: 'Dior affects mild surprise at the furore that has greeted his designs, for he considers them, as befits an introductory collection, to be simple and conservative. But to the fashion world, his long billowing shirts, high small waists, and narrow shoulders, are both revolutionary and immensely chic.'

Dior, it was said, also gave women back their natural shape. He actuated their breasts, rounded their hips and made their shoulders slender and feminine. Ironically, the curves of this 'natural' shape were completely artificial. A padded bra was required, along with a boned corset to give the nipped waist, and hip pads. The girdle-less wartime look, for all its drab severity, was more natural.

Dior's garments did not just hang on the body. They were constructed. Gowns were lined with taffeta and cambric to give them body and whale-bones were used to shape and curve the garments. The difference between Balenciaga's long padded jackets and Dior's was that Dior's stood out from the body. The curves were built in. His basques were rounded even when they were not on the model's figure. Slim models had to wear falsies to produced a rounder, more accentuated bustline. This had its downside. During the build-up to his first show, one of Dior's models fainted. He made a grab for her, and found he was left holding nothing but a pair of falsies.

But the most extraordinary thing about Dior's clothes – at a time when women were still wearing short, pleatless skirts, made to save fabric – was the sheer amounts of material in them. The grand centre-piece of the winter collection, Diorama, had a skirt forty metres in circumference. Unthinkable under the post-war rationing, it was everything every women craved.

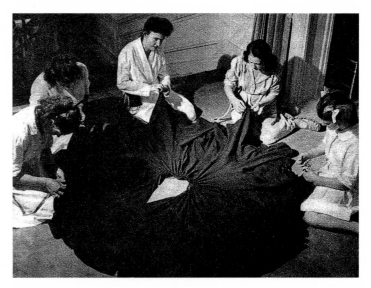

THE MAKING OF A DIOR

There was more to a Dior creation than acres of materials. Each and every garment was a labour of love. They were designed like a piece of architecture, resting on a foundation of hard-won dressmaking skills. Each dress was lined throughout and there were no darts.

'A well-cut dress is one with few cuts,' Dior said.

A hot iron was used to create the bustline. The bustier, or long-line brassiere, was part of the dress and was lined with two pieces of tulle lain in opposed directions. Most of the stitching was done by hand. In Dior's workshops, there were three sewing machines between forty women. Each garment need two or three fittings and took two-hundred hours of labour to complete. But the result as so well made that it would fit like a glove.

Dior, Spring '47:

Dress with neck-to-hem back buttoning

Dior, Spring '47:

All-pleated dress and safari hat

Dior, Spring '47:

The Gibson-Girl shirtwaist look

Dior, Spring '47:

Dress with kerchief back drapery

Dior, Spring '47:

Jacket with bow-knotted back belt

Dior, Spring '47:

Dress with barrel skirt and hip pleats

Dior, Spring '47:

Dress with bosom and skirt fan pleats

Dior, Spring '47:

Curved jacket and barrel skirt

A drawing which *Vogue* ran with the very first major piece about Dior in April 1947, it illustrates a dress called Maxime and was sketched at Maxim's, the Paris restaurant

The star of the first collection was an outfit called Bar. It had a jacket in natural shantung silk with a tailored collar and rounded basques, with pleated skirt of black wool. One of the dresses was called Corolla, which was also the name of the line and the collection. It was made of wool, collarless and fastened down the front of the bodice with five large buttons. The skirt had a plain centre panel. The rest of it was densely pleated and it was worn over petticoats. A similar skirt was employed in Chérie, but it had a gather through the pleats at hip level and the bodice had no sleeves. The principle colours were black, grey, marine blue and raw silk.

Not all the skirts were full. Passe-Partout was a tailored suit made in marine-blue crêpe wool with a slender skirt, as an alternative to the pleated ones. But it had no collar, pockets on the chest and a built-in basque. The sleeves were cuffed and the jacket only buttoned as far as the waist. The price was a whacking 30,000 francs.

Rita Hayworth bought the evening dress Soirée to wear to the premiere of her latest film *Gilda*. It had two tiers of pleated skirts in marine-blue taffeta. And she bought the trim-waisted suit Pompom, so called because its jacket and hem were trimmed with pompoms. It had a narrow skirt.

Susan Mary Patten, the wife of US diplomat William Patten, saw Dior's first collection. As a friend of one of the *vendeuses*, she was allowed into the fitting rooms after the show.

'This was more dangerous than entering a den of female lions before feeding time,' she later recalled. 'The richest ladies in Europe were screaming for the models, shrill cries of "Where is Miss New York?" I had it and someone has stolen it right from under my eyes.'

Meanwhile Daisy Fellowes re-asserted her place in Parisian society. The *vendeuses* from Dior showed her the collection in her magnificent apartment on the first floor of the Ritz.

However, Dior's New Look was not popular with the poor people of Paris.

'People shout *ordures* at you from vans because for some reason it creates class feeling in a way no sables could,' Nancy Mitford commented in a letter to Eddy Sackville-West. Even in a bistro in the 7th *arrondissement*, she recalled having to make excuses for her Dior outfit, explaining that she had been saving up the whole war for a new coat.

In March 1947, a photographic session turned into a riot. The photographer decided that Dior's New Look had to be presented in a recognisably Parisian setting, but using the Eiffel Tower or the Champs-Élysées as a background was considered too clichéed. Instead someone suggested the street markets of Montmartre.

The models put on their outfits in the back-room of a bar, then they walked out on to the Rue Lepic. The bustling street market fell silent. Suddenly a stall-holder let out an indignant shriek and launched herself at one of the models, screaming abuse. Another woman joined in. Together, they beat the model, tore at her hair and tried to rip the outfit off her. The models ran back into the bar, changed clothes and beat a hasty retreat back to the safety of Dior's salon.

'40,000 FRANCS FOR A DRESS AND OUR CHILDREN HAVE NO MILK.'

THE PROTEST

AFTER THE NEW LOOK WAS LAUNCHED, WOMEN DEMONSTRATED IN PARIS. THEY SHOUTED: '40,000 FRANCS FOR A DRESS AND OUR CHILDREN HAVE NO MILK.' IN 1947, DIOR'S GARMENTS WERE OUT OF REACH FOR ALL BUT THE WEALTHY. A SCHOOL TEACHER EARNED 9,000 FRANCS A MONTH AND OIL AND DAIRY PRODUCTS WERE STILL RATIONED. IN BRITAIN, THE PRESIDENT OF THE BOARD OF TRADE SAID THE LOOK WOULD REDUCE OUTPUT BY 800,000 GARMENTS AND URGED THE BRITISH GUILD OF CREATIVE DESIGNERS TO IGNORE IT. THE LABOUR GOVERNMENT CONSIDERED LEGISLATION TO GOVERN THE LENGTH OF SKIRTS.

MABEL RIDEALGH MP DECRIED THE STYLE, 'RIDICULOUS, STUPIDLY EXAGGERATED WASTE OF MATERIAL AND MANPOWER, FOISTED ON THE AVERAGE WOMAN TO THE DETRIMENT OF NORMAL CLOTHING. OUR MODERN WORLD HAS BECOME USED TO THE FREEDOM OF SHORT, SENSIBLE CLOTHING. THE NEW LOOK IS REMINISCENT OF A CAGED BIRD'S ATTITUDE. I HOPE OUR FASHION DICTATORS WILL REALISE THE NEW OUTLOOK OF WOMEN AND GIVE THE DEATH BLOW TO ANY ATTEMPT TO CURTAIL WOMEN'S FREEDOM.'

MRS BESSIE BRADDOCK MP CALLED THE NEW LOOK 'THE RIDICULOUS WHIM OF IDLE PEOPLE'. BUT SHE WAS MISREADING THE MOOD OF THE

TIME. EVERY WOMAN HANKERED FOR THE LUXURY OF A DIOR. MEN

WERE SICK OF SEEING WOMEN IN MEN'S CLOTHES, OR THE SEVERITY OF

THE UTILITY SUITS, AND PREFERRED DIOR'S FEMININE CREATIONS.

OTHER LEFT-WING COMMENTATORS DENOUNCED THE NEW LOOK AS A

RETURN TO THE DAYS WHEN 'FASHION WAS THE PREROGATIVE OF THE

LEISURED AND WEALTHY WOMAN AND NOT THE EVERYDAY CONCERN

OF THE TYPIST, SALESWOMAN OR HOUSEWIFE'. NOT MANY FELT THE

SAME. RADICAL INTELLECTUAL MARGHANITA LASKI TOLD BRITISH

VOGUE: 'PATRIOTISM IS DEFINITELY NOT ENOUGH AND, I, FOR ONE, AM

FED UP. I DON'T LIKE TO SEE A FOREIGNER POINTING AND WHISPERING

"YOU CAN SEE SHE IS ENGLISH – LOOK AT HER CLOTHES!"'

CENSORSHIP TRIED TO STOP THE NEW LOOK REACHING THE US. THERE

WERE PROTESTS BY WOMEN WHO ENJOYED THE FREEDOM OF CASUAL

CLOTHES. THEY PICKETED STORES WHERE THE NEW LOOK WAS SOLD

ONE WOMAN FOUNDED THE 'A LITTLE BELOW THE KNEE' CLUB, WHICH

ACQUIRED 1300 MEMBERS. THE SAN ANTONIO CHAPTER BOASTED: 'THE

ALAMO FELL, BUT OUR HEMLINES WILL NOT.' THERE WERE SOON MEM-

BERS IN ALL 48 STATES. THE GEORGIA LEGISLATURE ANNOUNCED ITS

INTENTION TO INTRODUCE A BAN ON LONG SKIRTS, WHILE CARTOONS

AND ARTISTS TRIED TO RIDICULE THE NEW LOOK OUT OF EXISTENCE.

**California members of
WOWS – the Womens
Organisation to War on
Styles – react to the long
skirt on the left by holding
their noses**

G MY WIFE,
AHO
ER FROM TEXAS WARNED:
E AND I'LL KICK YOU OUT.'

HOLLYWOOD DESIGNER ADRIAN JOINED BATTLE AGAINST THE NEW LOOK ON THE RADIO. BUT HE WAS SET AGAINST CARMEL SNOW OF *HARPER'S BAZAAR* AND EDNA WOOLMAN CHASE OF *VOGUE* WHO MORE ACCURATELY REFLECTED THE TIMES. AFTER YEARS OF WAR AND WORK, MANY WOMEN WANTED TO GO BACK TO THE HOME AND FAMILY. THEY CRAVED THE OPTIMISM AND OPULENCE NEW LOOK BROUGHT THEY WERE SICK OF THE L-85 DESIGNS, EVEN IF IT MEANT STABBING THE AMERICAN FASHION INDUSTRY IN THE BACK, THEY WERE HAPPY TO MAKE PARIS THE CENTRE OF THE FASHION WORLD AGAIN.

DIOR HIMSELF RECEIVED LETTERS FROM AROUND THE WORLD. MANY PRAISED HIM, OTHERS WERE CRITICAL. WHEN DIOR WENT TO AMERICA, PEOPLE MARCHED IN THE STREETS SHOUTING 'DOWN WITH THE NEW LOOK', AND 'BURN CHRISTIAN DIOR'. BUT HE WAS PREPARED. 'I KNOW I DESIGN FOR A SPECIAL CALLS OF WOMEN, THE ELEGANT OF THE WORLD BUT FASHION IS DEDICATED TO ALL THE WOMEN OF THE WORLD, TO WOMEN IN GENERAL. THERE IS NOTHING I WOULD LIKE BETTER THAN TO MAKE EVERY WOMAN LOOK AND FEEL LIKE A DUCHESS.'

IN FACT, DIOR LOVED TO SEE HIS DRESSES COPIED. SO THAT WOMEN WHO COULD NOT AFFORD HIS PRICES ALSO GOT THE PLEASURE OF BEING DRESSED BY DIOR.

These girls of the Anti-Long-Skirt Association of Dayton, Ohio, had an even more severe way of showing their dissaproval of the 'traitors who follow the dictates of Parisien fashion designers' – they took out their scissors and cut the garment back to a respectable knee-length!

Despite the reaction in the streets, Dior's New Look was a huge commercial success. It accounted for 75 per cent of the fashion export from France in 1947. Orders flooded in and Maison Dior had to open two additional workshops.

Part of the reason that Dior's New Look took off so speedily was the changes that had been made in the fashion industry during the war. In the 1930s, Paris couture houses had catered to a tiny minority of rich women. Their fashions had virtually no effect on the world at large. But the wartime streamlining of the ready-to-wear industry meant that Parisian couture fashions' licencees, quickly copied and made available to the general public at a fraction of the original cost.

In the autumn of 1947, Dior produced another *Corolla* line and also the *Back of Paris* line – which re-introduced the bustle, made out of gathers or bows, on evening dresses. Dior's backer, textile magnate Marcel Boussac, encouraged Dior to put even more fabric into his creations and *Elle* dubbed Dior's new line 'parachute skirts'. The models were told to spin around so that the huge shirts would billow out like flowers. In the programme notes, Dior again reinforced this message.

'The collection affirms the natural graces of Woman,' he wrote to his audience. 'Woman the stem, Woman the flower. The Corolla silhouette opens into a tulip, which is expressed more powerfully in the Diorama.'

Diorama was the star of the show. It was a black dress with one metre of material in the bodice and 20 metres in the skirt. The tiny bodice had short sleeves, a V-neck and tiny buttons to the waist.

On some coats and dresses, Dior dropped the hemline to the ankle 'to return the legs to all their mystery'. This harked back to 1916, to Dior's childhood and his memories of his mother. One of the long coats was called Mystère. It was in black cloth and with the collar and centre front of the skirt in eucalyptus green, pleated taffeta.

Other notable garments in Dior's next collection were Aladin, which was an afternoon dress with a collarless bodice, short sleeves decorated with knots and a black patent leather belt pinching the waist, and Bonbon, a black woollen shirt-waister with a pleated skirt that came down to only just below the calves. Bonbon was also available in pink.

Dior paid more attention to colour in his second collection. He did not entirely discard black and grey, but they were joined a range of reds, greens and pinks. Bright satins were used for evening dresses, designed to be worn under furs. Day dresses were longer, but evening dresses got slightly shorter, often with asymmetrical hemlines – something that Dior had avoided in his first collection.

Not a Dior, but an elegant
British New Look item in
Harper's, January 1948.
The suit, from Daley's of
Glasgow, cost £19.5s.3d,
that would be £19.26p in
decimal sterling

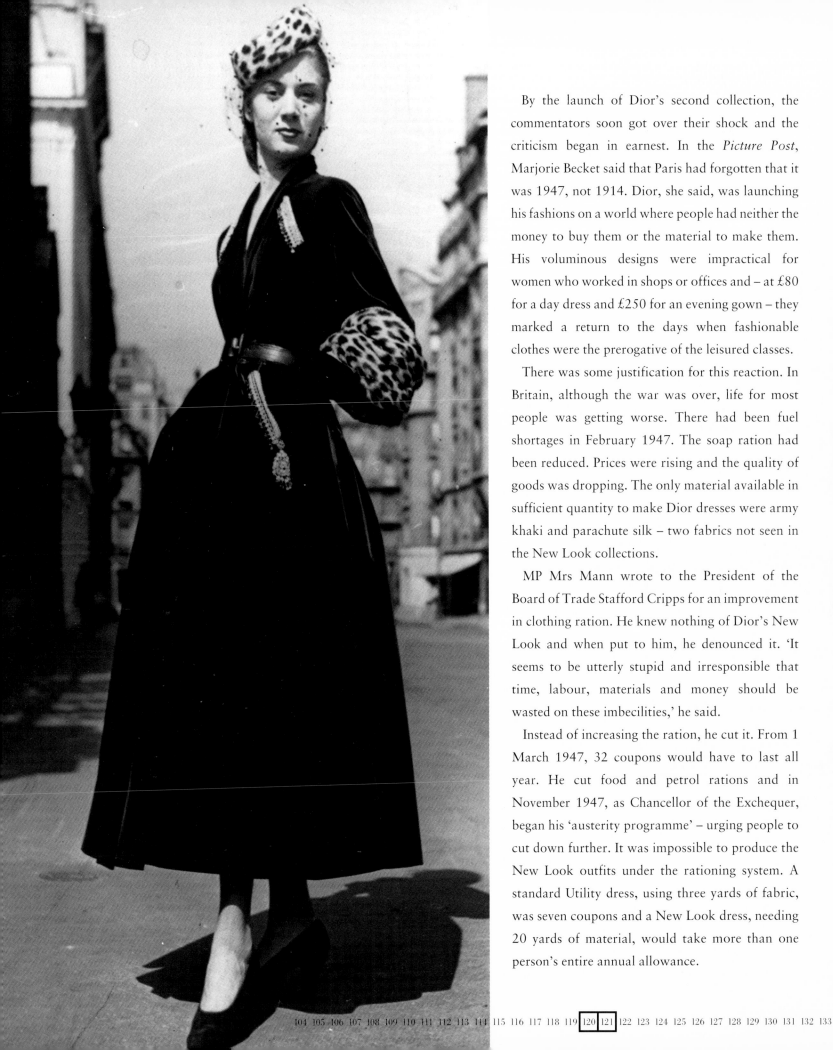

By the launch of Dior's second collection, the commentators soon got over their shock and the criticism began in earnest. In the *Picture Post*, Marjorie Becket said that Paris had forgotten that it was 1947, not 1914. Dior, she said, was launching his fashions on a world where people had neither the money to buy them or the material to make them. His voluminous designs were impractical for women who worked in shops or offices and – at £80 for a day dress and £250 for an evening gown – they marked a return to the days when fashionable clothes were the prerogative of the leisured classes.

There was some justification for this reaction. In Britain, although the war was over, life for most people was getting worse. There had been fuel shortages in February 1947. The soap ration had been reduced. Prices were rising and the quality of goods was dropping. The only material available in sufficient quantity to make Dior dresses were army khaki and parachute silk – two fabrics not seen in the New Look collections.

MP Mrs Mann wrote to the President of the Board of Trade Stafford Cripps for an improvement in clothing ration. He knew nothing of Dior's New Look and when put to him, he denounced it. 'It seems to be utterly stupid and irresponsible that time, labour, materials and money should be wasted on these imbecilities,' he said.

Instead of increasing the ration, he cut it. From 1 March 1947, 32 coupons would have to last all year. He cut food and petrol rations and in November 1947, as Chancellor of the Exchequer, began his 'austerity programme' – urging people to cut down further. It was impossible to produce the New Look outfits under the rationing system. A standard Utility dress, using three yards of fabric, was seven coupons and a New Look dress, needing 20 yards of material, would take more than one person's entire annual allowance.

Despite the controversy over the 'backward' trend of the New Look, full peg skirts, hourglass waists and sloping shoulders swept the USA. The items on this page and opposite were all by the American designer Paul Parnes

Nevertheless the New Look was unstoppable. In London, Dereta produced seven hundred New Look suits outside the Utility range in unrationed grey flannel. They sold out in two weeks.

The John Lewis Partnership held a New Look fashion show in 1947, but it was for members of staff only. Then, in 1948, the New Look first started to appear in the shops in Britain.

British *Vogue's* 'Choice of the Month' in June 1948 was one of the New Look suits in spotted rayon. It had a fitted jacket with basques, sloping shoulders, a hand-span waist and a flare shirt over a taffeta petticoat which came down over the calf. Though slimmer than the Dior original, it was available at Harvey Nichols in London, Bon Marché in Liverpool and MacDonald's in Glasgow for £15 6s 7d.

Fenwicks of Bond Street offered a 'ballerina suit' in the 'new fashion look' for £5 12s 6d and eighteen coupons. You were able to bear this shameless extravagance, the store pointed out, 'by wearing almost nothing underneath it'.

It was now inevitable that Utility would have to follow suit. In late September and October 1948, they put on a series of fashion shows in Welwyn Garden City. One of these featured a full-skirted afternoon dress in white, yellow and navy Italian tie silk. Though the hemline had dropped, the bodice retained the wartime square shoulders. It cost £5 17s 6d with seven coupons.

Also on show was a Harella Utility coat that cost £6 19s 6d with twelve coupons. It was double breasted with a moleskin collar. It was flared out in a wide, gored skirt below the calf but, again, retained the square shoulders.

HARPER'S

December *Bazaar*

**CHRISTMAS
AND YOUNG PEOPLE**

The New Look gets the
Royal assent in 1948
when the two Princesses,
Elizabeth and Margaret,
make an appearance at the
wedding of Lord Derby

Young women who wanted to follow the fashion
made New Look skirts out of blackout curtains. It
was the only material widely available.

Butterick Paper Patterns published a useful
method of making New Look dresses from old
ones. Women would take two old garments and
combine them to produce one New Look outfit.
And short dirndl skirts could be made longer by
unpicking the seams and turning them lengthwise.

The New Look presented the royal family with
a dilemma. King George VI's had two daughters,
Princess Elizabeth and Princess Margaret Rose.
They had to be seen obeying the restrictions, but
could not be seen to be anything but fashionable.
Molyneux stepped in to save the day. He added big
velvet bands to Princess Margaret's coat to widen
the skirt and lengthen the hem.

On the Continent, things were more austere, but
still clever young women found ways to keep up
with the fashion. In Holland, they made New Look
dresses out of patchwork, edged with the national
colour, orange. The shortages were so acute in the
Netherlands that they had to unpick old clothes to
make sewing thread. For a top, women wore ex-US
Army T-shirts, heralding the styles of the 1950s
and 1960s.

The continuing pressure of the Utility drive under post-
war rationing would seem in direct contradiction to the
need for longer lengths of material presented by the New
Look; here, at a London branch of Richards Shops, a
buyer demands a few more inches to keep up with fashion

In America, shortages were not a problem and the New Look immediately appealed to the young. They were offered full skirts, nipped-in jackets and 'bustle peplums'. Otherwise, though hemlines dropped, skirts remained slim, shoulders square, and hips and waistlines barely acknowledged.

Gradually though, Dior's New Look became accepted in smalltown America and it appeared in the pages of the Sears catalogue which attempted to recapture 1930s' Gibson Girl romanticism. Sears soon offered a jacket with a gold belt and junior dress that had a 110-inch rayon skirt. There was a moire skirt which was trimmed with ermine tails measuring 115 inches around the hem. Tears of ruffles edged cotton dresses, and the playclothes featured flaring skirts. 'Ballerina suits' made an appearance and sequins, beads and nailheads of new materials trimmed dresses.

To complement the new styles, there were flat ballerina and baby-doll shoes, though platform shoes with ankle straps worn with the new seamless stockings endured as an alternative.

In September 1947, Dior was invited to travel to the US to receive an award from Neiman-Marcus in Dallas. Dior insisted on sailing on the *Queen Mary* because of his love for all things British. He even loved English food – considered a strange thing for a Frenchman. But the Dior family was Norman and the people of Normandy are acutely aware of their ancient ties to England.

Dior was a shy man and, when he disembarked in New York, he found himself fielding intimidating questions from aggressive reporters. They accused him of hiding women's legs.

When they asked him what he thought of the 300,000 women would had joined the anti-Dior 'Little Below the Knee' club, Dior replied that those who protest the loudest will end-up wearing the longest skirts. He saw no reason to be apologetic.

Christian Dior faces the press aboard the *Queen Mary*, upon his arrival in New York in April 1948

An example of the 'tulip dress' in 1947, from the Autumn collection of an American design house

'I designed clothes for flowerlike women, with rounded shoulders, full, feminine busts, hand-span waists above enormous spreading skirts,' he said later. 'I brought back the art of pleasing.'

'I BROUGHT BACK THE ART OF PLEASING.' Christian Dior

Another outfit by the US designer Paul Parnes, a day coat in scarlet broadcloth worn over a black wool princess dress

A wonderful example of a New Look Utility suit in a UK *Vogue* article in June 1948 titled 'Smart Fashions For Limited Incomes'

Dior in the fitting room with some of his models, 1950

Dior the Artist

Christian Dior was born on 21 January 1905 in a large pink and grey house with a high-walled garden overlooking the Channel, in the seaside resort of Granville, Normandy. The second of five children, he had two sisters and two brothers. His father, Alexandre Dior, ran the family firm which manufactured chemical fertilisers. It had been founded in the 1832 by Dior's great-great-grandfather.

The family were well off. Early pictures show Christian in an English sailor suit; very much in fashion after the establishment of the Anglo-French *entente cordiale* in 1904. In 1910, the Dior family moved to Paris, though they returned to Granville every year for holidays. The move was a wrench for young Christian, who always hated change.

Dior's early education was in the hands of a German governess, Madame Lefebvre. When he was eleven he was sent to school at Gerson. His school books were filled with sketches of women's legs in high-heeled shoes.

In his early teens, Christian Dior appeared as King Neptune at a fancy dress party in Granville casino. This marked the beginning of a lifelong love of clothes and dressing up.

In 1919, Dior went to a charity bazaar in aid of soldiers, dressed as a gypsy. There, a fortune teller read his hand. She told him one day he would find himself without money, but that women were his destiny. They would give him great success.

In his late teens, Dior was showing some artistic flair and, like Pierre Balmain and Digby Morton, he wanted to become an architect. He toyed with the idea of going to art school, but his family were determined that he go into some more respectable profession. They thought that he should join the diplomatic corp and in 1923 he was sent to the Ecoles des Science Politiques.

But this did not quash his artistic ambitions. While at diplomatic school, he began composing music and mixing in artistic circles. He even wrote a ballet, which was performed in the 1940s.

Dior graduated with a BSc in political science in 1926. The following year he was called up for national service. When he was discharged, he told his family that he had decided to give up the Quai d'Orsay for Montmartre and open an art gallery.

His father was particularly disappointed. But he backed his son and put up the money for the gallery, provided the family name did not appear on the shop front. Dior struck up a partnership with Jean Bonjean and the Galerie Bonjean opened at 34 Rue La Boetie in Paris in 1928.

It exhibited the most avant garde paintings of the time, including work by Picasso, Braque, Chirico, Utrillo, Léger and Dufy. The gallery also provided a centre for Dior's increasingly fast and bohemian life.

'It was a question of running as fast as possible, in order not to miss a single preview or party, but rather to enjoy the unique privilege of being at one with the century in committing the follies of youth. The privilege of dancing at all hours, whatever the cost, of staying awake all night, of listening to negro music, of carefree awakenings, or drunken revels devoid of nausea, of light-hearted love affairs and serious friendships; but above all else it was the privilege of "being available". We were "available" then as people are "otherwise engaged" today. I took advantage of this watchword to explore the whole of Paris, a Paris that was new and inventive, cosmopolitan and intelligent, and prodigal of all that was genuinely new.'

Dior spent much of his time with art dealers. Modern art still had an air of black mass about it. And black was in vogue at that time. The business thrived despite Dior's casual attitude to it. He was supported by luminaries, Jean Cocteau and Max Jacob, together with Christian Bérard, Pierre Gaxotte and Henri Sauguet.

It was then that tragedy struck. In 1931, Dior's elder brother Raymonde succumbed to a terrible fatal illness. Dior's mother died soon after. He had always been very close to her. To cope with his grief, he took a trip with a party of architects to the USSR. There he fell in love with the sensual shapes of the Russian Orthodox churches.

When Dior returned to France in 1932, the great Depression had struck. His father was ruined and Dior was forced to sell the gallery. The cosy world of his youth was gone forever.

For two years, Dior made ends meet by helping out at Pierre Collé's gallery. This was where he met Salvador Dali. Another artist, Jean Ozenne, taught Dior the art of fashion drawing. The American designer Max Kenna instructed him on the use of colour. And in 1933, Dior managed to sell his first hat designs to Agnès.

Dior lived quite well, with help from his friends. They invited him to parties and restaurants at their expense. But as most of them lived in hotels, there was no way they could put him up. He found some shelter in a condemned building. The roof leaked and his garret had neither water or electricity.

In 1934, Dior was struck down by tuberculosis. His friends clubbed together and sent him to the Balearic Islands to convalesce. There, he learnt tapestry weaving. When he returned to Paris in 1935, he moved in with Jean Ozenne and Max

Kenna helped him sell his designs to the couture houses at twenty francs a time. He was encouraged by the editor of *Vogue* Michael de Brunhoff and the interior designer George Geffroy. Between 1935 and 1938, he designed for Agnès, Schiaparelli, Molyneux, Balenciaga, Nina Ricci, Patou, Maggy Rouff, Paquin and Worth.

From 1936 on, his drawings appeared in *Le Figaro*. Soon he was earning enough to move into his own apartment at 10 Rue Royale in Paris, almost opposite Maison Molyneux, which was at number 5.

Although Dior had become a skilled draftsman, he still knew nothing about making clothes. In 1938, Georges Geoffrey introduced him to the couturier Robert Piguet, who then took him on as a *modéliste*. At Piguet's, Dior learnt all about the construction of clothes. Soon he decided to become a couturier himself and, courtesy of Piguet, began to learn everything he could about the business.

Dior designed three collections at Piguet's salon. One of them features 'amphora' dresses, which emphasised and rounded women's hips. But their time was yet to come. His most famous creation for Piguet was Café Anglais, a day-time hound's-tooth dress with a short, full skirt over a linen petticoat. It turned out to be the greatest success of the season. The designer Christian Bérard soon sought out the creator of Café Anglais.

'It was then that I knew I had arrived,' said Dior.

Dior also started designing costumes for theatre, dressing productions of Sheridan's *School for Scandal* and Jean Planchon's *Captain Smith* in the period costume of the Second Empire, complete with bustles and crinolines.

In August 1939, Dior was called up. He was an anti-militarist by nature and he was an anarchist by inclination. He refused to train as an officer and became a private first class at Génie, but he actually saw very little action.

After the armistice was signed on 25 June 1940, Dior was demobbed and he went to stay with his father and sister who had a farm at Callian in Provence. They grew peas and green beans, and travelled on foot to sell them in Cannes. They only made it to the first harvest because unexpectedly, Dior received a cheque for a thousand dollars from America, for some of the last paintings that had been sold from his gallery.

For the next eighteen months, Dior worked as a market gardener. In this strange world a million miles from the urban milieu he was used to, he found that he liked the land and loved nature.

But Dior could not leave fashion behind him. He contacted *Le Figaro* and provided them with fresh sketches. Then, in December 1941, he went back to Paris. However, he had delayed too long. Piguet had already taken on a new designer, Castillo.

Penniless again, Dior poured out his troubles to a friend, Paul Caldaguès. Caldaguès introduced Dior to Lucian Lelong, who immediately took him on.

In Lelong's designed studio, Dior worked with Pierre Balmain, who had trained with Molyneux. And it was at Lelong that Dior learnt the methods of Maison Molyneux.

Dior also designed for the film industry at that time. Under Nazi control, French film makers were heavily censored and costume dramas were the safest bet. Dior went back to designing bustles and crinolines for the actress Odette Joyeux, who he had dressed for the stage. He took great pains to make his creations authentic. He closely studied the construction of eighteenth- and nineteenth-century clothes in museum archives. He was particularly interested in the dresses that Charles Frederick

Worth had made for some of the empresses of France, Austria and Russia.

Balmain left to set up on his own in 1944, leaving Dior in charge of design at Lelong. By spring 1946, he was already experimenting with some of the major ideas of the New Look – sloping shoulders, nipped-in waists and full skirts.

In summer 1946, Dior was walking in the streets of Paris when he bumped into an old friend from Granville, who was the managing director of the dressmakers Philippe et Gaston.

Philippe et Gaston were an old established firm who needed a new designer to breathe life back into the company. Dior's friend asked if he knew of anybody to fit the bill. Dior did not respond. They met three times on the pavement between Rue Saint Forentine and Rue Royale, where Dior lived, before Dior put his own name forward.

The owner of the firm was cotton magnate Marcel Boussac. He was the son of a successful draper who had left him £70,000 in order for him to set up his own textile business in 1909. During the First World War, Boussac supplied the French army with cloth for their uniforms and webbing. After the armistice, he bought back the huge surplus of cloth the French and British armies now had and started producing cheap clothing. He became a millionaire and was a familiar figure at the race courses.

During the Depression he remained solvent and expanded his empire buying bankrupt companies. In the 1930s, he became France's largest cotton spinner and weaver, helped by France's trading laws which prevented the French colonies from importing foreign textiles.

Dior met Boussac, but told him frankly that he would not take over Philippe et Gaston. The staff were too old and established. They would resist any new ideas. Besides, he did not want to work for another house. Balmain had already set up on his own and he wanted to do the same.

Dior explained that he had ideas of his own that he wanted to try out, free from the interference of Lelong or any other couturier. He wanted to set up on his own, in a small house dressing just a few sophisticate elegant women, in the best tradition of *haute couture*.

Then Dior got carried away. He told Boussac that, now the war was over, new fashion was waiting to burst out. With a new fashion house he would be in a perfect position to take advantage of the post-war boom that was coming. His garments would look simple but be highly elaborate. He wanted to make long, full skirts with plenty of petticoats, like his mother had worn when he was a child.

Boussac sat up when he heard this. Longer, fuller skirt and petticoats meant the use of more fabric. If Dior could make them fashionable, it would give the textile industry a much-need fillip.

Boussac offered Dior ten million francs to start up his own fashion house. But Dior panicked. He had never run a business before. He broke off the negotiations with Boussac's right-hand man Henri Fayolle and ran straight to his fortune-teller Madame Delahaye. She told him: 'All that may be offered to you later is as nothing compared to the chance you have here today.'

Dior was deeply superstitious. His lucky number, he believed, was eight. The letter M, the lily of the valley and stars were also sources of good fortune for him. A second clairvoyant was consulted. She went into a trance and declared: 'This house will revolutionise fashion.'

'This confirmation of one clairvoyant by another finally gave me the strength to act,' Dior wrote later.

From *Vogue* 1947, a tussore jacket and pleated skirt by Dior drawn by the legendary illustrator Christian Berard who died just two years later

But Boussac was a shrewd businessman and knew better than to leave ten million francs in the hands of an amateur. He installed one of his own business managers, Jacque Rouët, as director general. Dior would be artistic director, responsible for design and production, while Rouët would keep a reign on the money.

When Dior first met Rouët, he insisted that Rouët change his hat. The one he had on, he claimed, was quite impossible. But otherwise Dior felt that Rouët was the man for the job.

Although Dior acted naive about business, with his family background, he actually understood about investments, manufacturing and running costs. But Dior's artistic side made him extremely temperamental. This was not helped by the fact that he surrounded himself by women who mothered him and indulged his every whim.

In this charged atmosphere, Rouët remained even tempered. He was firm and diplomatic, and could force through savings and rationalisations against all opposition. Even though Boussac produced all the material Dior could want, Rouët insisted on buying in shantung which was very cheap from China. The most famous outfit in the New Look collection – Bar – had a Chinese shantung jacket.

The new company was registered in October 1946. In December, Dior resigned from Lelong – after agreeing to design two more collections for him and to supervise their manufacture. He took a five-floor mansion at 30 Avenue Montaigne, in the smart 8th *arrondissement* between the Champs Elysées and the Seine. This was out of the *haute couture* district, but was still fashionable. Christian Bérard designed the boutique, while Victor Grandpierre was chosen to handle the decor. Dior insisted that the interiors be grey, like Molyneux's house in Rue Royale. Grey, he felt, gave the rooms a restrained ambience which would not conflict with the clothes. But he did not chose the pearl grey that Molyneux had. He opted for shades of light and dark grey, outlined in white.

Instead of the grey uniforms Molyneux staff wore, Dior's sales staff were dressed in traditional black, while those in the workrooms wore white overalls. There were three workrooms at Dior's and 85 staff. Marguerite Carré was in charge in the workrooms and was responsible for turning Dior's drawings into clothes. She had been at Patou for eighteen years and brought her own staff of thirty. Raymonde Zehnacker, the storekeeper at Lelong's, was in charge of the studio. The stylist was Germaine 'Mitzah' Bricard, who had been with Molyneux. She also ran the hat department.

Other staff came by word of mouth. In fact, the whole fashion world was buzzing with what was happening at Dior. Usually, when designers set up as couturiers, they made a precarious start. Few knew how to manage a business and scraped along trying to make ends meet until they had enough money for a business manager. But here was Dior, backed by fifty million francs, with a business manager in place.

Lida and Zika Ascher were soon at his door and sold him some silks for his first collection. Graham Sutherland, Henry Moore and other leading artists designed scarves to be sold in the boutique. Seven mannequins were taken on and everyone worked overtime to produce the first collection.

Dior planned ninety dresses for that first show and claimed he had no idea what he was about to unleash on the world. He said all he wanted to do was to become a 'good tailor'. When he saw the reaction to his collection, he was heard to mutter: 'What have I done? What on earth have I done?'

Employees of the House of Dior in Paris read of his death in Italy on 24th October, 1957

THE TRIUMPHANT

NEW

THE

LOOK

Above, a Dior dress with a
wing-back *decolleté*, 1948

Previous page, an evening
gown by Dior on the steps
of the Paris Opera, 1948

Right, Dior evening dress
from Autumn 1951

Left, a Dior dress with the
Envol or *Flight* line which
he launched in 1948

Right, Dior's *Long* line of
1951 gave the illusion of
greater length to the body

'From the New Look to the Now Look' was how *Harper's* headlined this spread of comparisons between the *haute couture* collections of 1947 and 1948

They compared accessories (above) where handbag and umbrella had given way to a fur stole, and hats (left) – 'last season's was a wide shovel, this season's is a cone'

Right: 'Last season's dress was strapless and bare. This season's dress is strapless, too, but you shroud your shoulders in a scarf or a shawl of chiffon or cobwebby lace'

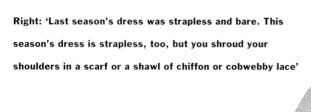

This 1948 action shot of a Dior model in full twirl was taken by the renowned Magnum photographer Robert Capa

In spring 1948, all the Paris fashion houses were showing 'New Look' collections. France's capital was overflowing with voluptuous figures. Waists were minute. All hips, bosoms and *derrières* were padded. Shoulders were dropped, sleeves were dolman or raglan with some underarm fullness and skirts had dropped to seven or eight inches off the ground. And London and New York had, once again, to ceded pre-eminence in the fashion world to Paris.

Dior showed his *Zig Zag* and *Flight* lines. The *Zig Zag* line had an over-skirt with panels with sloping hems. These were turned back on themselves, which created a Z shape against the skirt beneath.

The *Flight* line had narrow skirts and fly-out jackets, stiffed with buckram, which flared out over the waist. Aventure was a prime example, featuring a narrow black dress in a woollen cloth and a jacket with the back was flared out with godets in chicken's-foot yellow.

In evening wear, Dior continued his bustle effect. Typical of the collection was Martinique, which had a strapless corsage over an ankle-length skirt in striped organza. The front panel pleated from the waist, while a longer panel of pleats at the back recalled the dresses of the late nineteenth century.

In May 1948, Princess Margaret visited Paris, wearing a British version of the New Look by Molyneux. This was immediately dubbed the 'London Look'. Molyneux' waists were narrow. His skirts were not as full as Dior's and his hemlines came down just below the calf – by then, Dior had dropped his to the ankle. According to Nancy Mitford, Dior did not approve

'The London New Look made me die laughing,' she wrote. 'Literal chintz crinolines. Apparently Dior went over: and when he reflected on the fact that he was responsible for launching it, he was ready to kill himself.'

Dior the Man

In 1947 Christian Dior was an unlikely revolutionary; forty-one, stout, grey-haired and balding, he had the bearing of a gentleman. Immaculately dressed by the finest tailors, he bore none of the outward signs of the artist. Nor did he conform to the image of homosexual designer. He liked to look at women – though, it was said, to dress them rather than undress them. He was deeply conservative, hated change and sought to protect himself from the outside world. He liked walled gardens, slept in four-poster beds with closed

A portrait of Christian Dior taken in 1954. At forty-nine he hardly looked a revolutionary – he was stout, grey-haired and balding, with the refined bearing of a gentleman.

curtains and surrounded himself with maternal women. Although a private man, he had many good friends and loved food, music and parlour games – his only slip from the pinnacle of sophistication.

The drawing room, one of the lavish interiors of Dior's Paris house, with *Sèvres jardinière* and Aubusson carpet

However, beneath the benign exterior there lurked a violent temper. His usually gentle nature could crack with a tantrum of unbelievable fury.

After the success of the New Look Dior bought a Louis XIV house in Boulevard Jules Sandeau. It was decorated in impeccable style by Pierre Delbée, Georges Geffroy and Victor Grandpierre, with quilted upholstery, silks and wall-hangings and silver taps. Outside there was a winter garden.

He bought the most expensive furniture and lived in high style with a Spanish butler to dress him, while his chef produced exquisite foods (especially desserts), served faultlessly.

Dior also bought and converted a windmill at Coudret where he indulged his love of nature. He had the local marshland drained and laid down an English lawn and got his eccentric Polish gardener, Ivan, to create carpets of flowers. He waded around in sewer boots, deciding where best to plant a willow, experimented with vegetables and flowers and tried, in vain, to improve the fruit trees.

In 1955, Molyneux bought a flower farm in the South of France. Dior bought one too – Colle Noire at Montauroux. There he planted vines and jasmine and raised carnations, added a pond and altered and extended the house so much that in the

In sharp contrast with his Paris home, the simple austerity of Dior's old mill house – his *Moulin* – at Milly, near Fontainbleau

end it resembled a Roman villa. Dior spent his last summer there, and would pop over to have lunch with Molyneux. A reporter from a newspaper in Nice once wrote of the visits of the 'Emperor of Couture' to the 'Pope of Mode'. Yet during their meetings they did not discuss clothes – but flowers, Molyneux told Dior he would be happy to provide any advice on running his flower farm.

'Paris In The Spring' was
how *Harper's* headlined
Dior's sensational evening
dress of pink chiffon (left)

From the same article of
April 1949, Dior's black
faille dinner dress (right)

Nevertheless for his autumn collection Dior did follow suit, raising his hemlines to 14 inches off the ground. *Harper's Bazaar* cheered, though Dior tried to hide the fact that he was now following the fashion rather than leading it by claiming, in his programme notes, that the interest that season was no longer in the length of skirts.

That autumn, he introduced the *Winged* line and the *Cyclonic* line. The *Winged* line followed from the *Flight* line and introduced a winged shape to sleeves and skirt. One dress, Coquette, had a winged bustle, reminiscent of the 1870s. The *Cyclonic* line, the programme notes said, 'tried to freeze the impact of a cyclone on a dress'. One of the *Cyclonic* dresses, Giroutte, or the Weathercock – had a strapless bodice made of black velvet and a black taffeta shirt which was held permanently in huge folds by horsehair reinforcement.

Dior went his own way in hats though. Mitzah Bricard discarded the cartwheels Princess Margaret had been wearing and promoted a line of smaller, more understated hats. These required a change in hairstyle and the ballerina Zizi Jeanmaire pioneered the *gamine* look with hair just three inches long. In Britain, this was known as the 'urchin cut'.

In the following year the 'tulip cut' came in, which was almost indisguishable from a pudding basin – and it was thought 'terribly amusing' to have a blonde bun on a brunette head of hair.

In February 1948, Dior introduced his *Trompe L'Oeil*, or *Illusion* line, and his *Foreign* line. The hemlines stayed where they were, while this time Dior covered his creations in false pockets. The central illusion was layers of petals sewn on evening skirts, which fluttered when the wearer moved. Suits lost their tailored collars.

Nobody could quite work out which country these 'Foreign' jackets and suits were supposed to have come from, but the Magyar was the most obvious inspiration.

Dior's use of colour was the most obvious change that spring. He had just moved into the countryside at Coudret and his collection incorporated the colours of grass, wheat and flowers, particularly the white of lilies of the valley, which was Dior's favourite flower.

Dior at Work

Dior produced two new lines a season – four a year – from 1947 until 1951. After this he cut back to two a year. In his ten years of designing under his own name he had produced thirty new lines of clothes.

He always worked in the same way. He began with the fabric. Usually he would pick from the samples offered by manufacturers. Appointments would be made every 15 minutes. Fabric makers would turn up to find Dior sitting at the middle of a long table, surrounded by his minions. He would pick up the samples and fondle them. Then he would push the ones he did not like to the right and those he had selected to the left. With these, he would ask for a length to be sent on approval.

Occasionally he made suggestions himself. The Swiss cloth-maker Madama Brossin de Méré produced Saintegallette for him, which is said to capture the colours of the roofs of Saint Gall.

Once he had chosen his fabrics, Dior would go off on holiday or spend time in the country to clear his mind. Then he would start making tiny sketches. He would sketch everywhere – in the bath, in bed, at the dinner table, in the car. All the time he would be trying to capture an emotion, a line or a movement.

When he saw something emerging, he would make a larger drawing, working up particular themes. Then he would put then aside. After a week, he would get it out again and simplify and distil the theme. Then, in just a few days, he would produce hundreds of drawings working up a dozen ideas.

At this stage he would return to the Avenue Montaigne, where he worked in a large bright studio. Wearing a white smock, he would closet himself with three women – Marguerite Carré, who had poached from Patou, Raymonde Zehnacker, who he had brought with him from Lelong, and Germaine 'Mizza' Bricard, who had once been a *demi-mondaine* – that is, an expensive prostitute.

'Nowadays,' she was heard saying, 'society women have brought the profession into disrepute. They'll go to bed for a *café crème*.'

Madame Bricard was moody, excessive and perpetually late. She never rose before two in the afternoon and wore a new dress everyday. But Dior saw her has the epitome of urban sophistication. She was his muse.

The four of them would go through the sketches and cut them down to around sixty, reflecting a dozen themes. Marguerite Carré would then take them to the seamstresses who would run them up as linen toiles.

Dior would sit in armchair, armed with a gold-tipped cane, while the entire collection was paraded in front of him. He would use just three models, usually brunettes of average height which he picked himself. He adored his models and was criticised for paying them too much. But he found inspiration in his models, especially those who could breathe life into a gown at toile stage.

'My models – they are the life of my dresses, and I want my dresses to be happy,' he would say.

Dior would then make a final selection of five or six lines, with their variations. Then he would review each toile in turn, chose a fabric for it and chose which girl would model it.

Although Dior started with the fabric, he did not match the fabric to the dress until the end of the process. His clothes were always more about shape than texture or colour. His task, he believed, was to 'construct a

Dior's 'muse', but certainly not the only lady in his life, the latter-day courtesan Germaine 'Mizza' Bricard

Stocking were a feature of Dior's Spring collection of 1948. They came in a range of colours from soft pink to ink black, called 'Boulevard Bouquet'

Dior backstage with one of his eight mannequins at the Gleneagles, Scotland, charity fashion show and ball, May 1955

When models were called
mannequins: Dior enjoys
posing with seven of the
world's most beautiful –
and certainly most
photographed – women

Watching from the wings,
the master awaits his
entrance to join the
models at the Gleneagles
charity event

series of volumes, proportionate to the female figure, in such a way as to highlight its forms'. His collection, he said, could equally well be designed in black and white. In the vital choice of fabric, colour was almost irrelevant. He was much more concerned with weight, thickness, suppleness and firmness, and would spend hours chosing between thirty high-quality black woollen fabrics.

However, every collection had to have one red dress – Dior believe that red was his lucky colour. Most of his dresses were black though 'The violent accent of black makes it the most elegant colour,' he said.

Once the fabric was chosen, it was time to name the dresses and have them made up. The finished dresses would then be announced to the maestro theatrically. Dior and the seamstresses would work on the dress on the model herself, shifting the neckline, lengthening it or shortening, shifting a seam by a centimetre. Thirty models would then be paraded in the Grand Salon and Dior would pick which ones were to be the prototype of his next new line.

A collection would consist of up to 175 outfits with coats to go with them. There would be fixed number of suits, day dresses, evening gowns and coats. Work would continue on the trimmings until the final rehearsal, which itself would drag on sometimes to midnight. By this time Dior would be delighted by his own work. As the models paraded by he would mutter: 'How pretty she is. Couldn't be better dressed. Couldn't be more elegant.'

His acolytes would echo his thoughts, comparing his creations to paintings – which is seen as the highest praise in *haute couture*. The problem of this way of working was the Dior was protected from criticism. He was surrounded by flock of motherly ladies who cosseted him. The French press would rarely question the words of the master and the only genuine criticism he would receive would come occasionally from Molyneux and Balmain.

However, Dior was aware of the problem and his self-congratulation at the rehearsal was superficial. By the morning of the show, he would be consumed by anxiety.

Attendance at the show was by invitation only. Some three hundred people would be invited. Buyers had to pay a deposit, which was forfeit if they failed to place an order. Security was tight. Dior was terrified of his designs being stolen and he once physically ejected a women who he saw sketching one of his dresses.

The salon manager was Suzanne Luling, a childhood friend of Dior's from Granville. The two of them would draw up a list of rich and famous women they wanted to dress. They were invited. Few failed to show up. They almost all placed orders – and they came back.

Dior employed fifty experienced saleswomen. They were told never to rush a client.

'Let her go elsewhere,' Susan Luling would say. 'She'll come back in the end.'

And they did.

Dior never attended fittings. But on one occasion he heard an important client rudely berate one of his seamstresses. Dior could not tolerate rudeness and, when he heard the customer's tone of voice, he actually asked her to leave.

A drawing of a Dior dress – 'le Chapeau Bleau' – by the most famous of fashion illustrators René Gruau, from a 1949 edition of the French *Fémina* magazine

In a savage-looking Pierre Cardin lion costume, Christain Dior at the fancy dress ball given by the Comte de Beamont, Paris 1947

Dior's autumn collection in 1949 brought the *Scissor* and the *Windmill-in-the-Wind* line. *Harper's Bazaar* dubbed it the 'vol-au-vent' look because of his use of flying panels. These panels crossed over each other like the scissor blades or the blades of a windmill. The effect was further emphasised by using contrasting materials – velvet was set against wool, satin against velvet, cloth against satin. But the press particularly picked up on the huge shawl collars on coats, which were full and loose. Dior explained that he had drawn inspiration from the rough cloaks worn by shepherds.

Several *Illusion* dresses from the spring collection had been held back until autumn. Peruvian was a black satin evening gown, covered with black satin leaves and clusters on the upper arm. Venus had petal shapes in pink tulle and a train of petals and leaves, all embroidered. And Juno had large petals covered in embroidered sequins around the hem.

Up to this point, there had been no concerted resistance to the New Look. This was because the other rising star of *haute couture*, Pierre Balmain, was recuperating in Australia after an accident, when Dior had launched it. But in 1949, Balmain was well again and responded with his *Oriental* line. He followed up with a back-to-the-1920s line, which was a big flop. By then it was already too late. The New Look had taken off world-wide.

Clothes rationing in Britain ended officially in April 1949. It was announced by the then President of the Board of Trade Harold Wilson, who publicly tore up his own ration book. But even this was an empty gesture. The great forces of fashion had already outflanked the old Utility scheme. The New Look outfits were already in all the stores. Paquin, Piguet, Fath, Craven and Dessès all followed the new silhouette. In 1950, they formed themselves into the Couturiers Associés and did business with the John Lewis Partnership.

Thanks to Dior Paris was regaining its reputation as the capital of high fashion. To celebrate, in 1949, Comte Etienne de Beaumont staged the 'ball of kings and queens', a fancy dress ball, with Dior as guest of honour. Dior went as a lion – the king of the beasts – with a lion's head made out of papier maché, an evening dress covered in fake orders of chivalry and a long cloak. The outfit was designed by Pierre Cardin who had just left Maison Dior after two years to set up on his own. He opened his own theatrical costumiers.

From *Vogue*, April 1949,
a dress described as
'Dior's dramatic surah;
skirt spiralling from above-
knee to train-length. Stiff
pockets form bodice'

Spencer, one of Dior's important lines of 1951, with oval neck, oval sleeves and oval hips

Princess Margaret in the ballgown designed by Dior for her 21st birthday which she celebrated at Balmoral, and pictured here in a photograph by Cecil Beaton

The orders of chivalry did not remain fake for long though. In 1950, Dior was awarded the Légion d'Honneur by a grateful French government. Almost single-handedly he had revived one of France's most lucrative export businesses.

Dior was at last getting the recognition in his own country that he had already secured all around the rest of the world. In just two short years, he had completely restructured women. The Duchess of Windsor – always a fashion setter – had expressed doubts about the New Look to start with. Now she was a client of Dior's. The prima ballerina Margot Fonteyn had bought the Daisy suit from his first collection. And when Molyneux retired in 1950, Princess Margaret turned to Dior.

And still the New Look rolled on. In 1950, Dior introduced the *Vertical* line. Bodices were moulded like sweaters. They were often sleeveless with plunging necklines to emphasise the bust. This Dior called the horseshoe neckline. Generally, the look was narrowed with pleats being kept within the line of the hips. But there were voluminous dust-coats made from panels of shantung set at right angles to the line of the fabric.

The horseshoe neckline was also used on bolero or Spencer jackets in suits. Navy blue and white was used on daywear and the straw boater made an appearance. These fashions again seemed to echo the sailor suits that Dior remembered from his childhood in Normandy.

His gowns for early evening were short – calf length – while grand evening dress incorporated embroidery and brocades. Organza, georgettes, taffetas and muslins, all in silk, were given a radical new treatment. Ribbons appeared on pleated muslin, giving a ray effect. This collection included another curiosity – an umbrella hat which could collapse and be put in the pocket.

Autumn 1950 saw the introduction of the *Oblique* line. It used raised collars rather like an architectural pediment. The general shape of the collection was narrow at the top and wide at the bottom, looking forward to Dior's *A* line. The new *Lily-of-the-Valley* line, introduced at the same time, also had day dresses that widened at the base.

In spring 1951, Dior reverted to a more natural look, though he emphasised the oval of the bust and hips. Sleeves were cut in what Dior call the 'chicken's thigh' – wide and the top and narrowed at the elbow. But strapless evening gowns, tightly moulded around the bust and hips, with full shirts persisted. Princess Margaret ordered for her 21st birthday, a ballgown from this collection. It was made in white silk organza with one shoulder strap on the left shoulder and front panel embroidered with flowers and foliage in straw tone, spangles and mother of pearl.

Dior announced the *Long* line in autumn 1951 which, he said, ended 'the evolution inherited from previous collections'. Basques were removed from suit jackets to make the skirt seem longer. The style inspired by the *Directoire* and *Empire* periods in France, but Dior did not copy the classical high waist. And although the even gowns of the *Empire* period avoided waistlines, Dior still flared the skirts New Look-style. Again the *Long* line can seen to be another move towards the *A* line.

Right, a 1951 Dior gown; behind, the Palace of Versailles
Below, a 1953 Dior Edwardian-styled black satin ball dress

THE PRICE

The price of Dior outfits was generally a matter decided between the couturier and his customers. But in April 1955, there was a show of Dior gowns in aid of the National War Memorial Health Foundation in South Africa. Evening gowns were valued between £195 and £950. A Dior fur coat was priced at £4,000, and a bridal gown had a price tag of £55,000.

Buyers paid a surcharge of 40 to 50 per cent on each model, which gave them the right to copy the garment. They took it without trying it on and often in the form of a toile or paper pattern.

The whole business of selling distressed Dior. He hated to see his creations fought over roughly by the buyers. Once the collection was shown, the applause and hugs and kisses over, he would leave.

Opposite, the long
moulded line of Dior's 'red
pepper' outfit, with a dress
and coat in the same
weight silky-surface
woollen. The nickname
came from the cap which
is like the top of a pepper,
complete with stalk

Near right, 'Belotte', a
grey tweed suite typical of
Dior's large jacket and
slim skirt 1953 creations

Far right, also from 1953,
Dior's dress and jacket
'afternoon' ensemble
which he called 'Sabine'

By this time Dior was using Molyneux as his consultant. Dior was a revolutionary, while Molyneux believed in evolution. His advice had always been not to introduce a new look overnight. It upset the industry. Molyneux believed that a designer should think ahead and hint at where he is going season by season. It was plainly advice that Dior was beginning to follow.

The *Sinuous* line came in spring 1952. Shoulders lost their shaping and corseting was abandoned. Waists rose to *Empire* levels, or sank to the hips. Women had changed shape from a flower to a stalk.

Autumn 1952 saw the launch of the chemise dress and evening dresses began to slim down, though hems were dropped four inches from his previous collection. A new long-line girdle gave Dior's models a slimmer silhouette. He featured leopard prints, which appeared in *Elle* magazine and Anita Loos' *Gentlemen Marry Brunettes*

(1955), the follow up to *Gentlemen Prefer Blondes* (1953). In the movie Jeane Crain and Jane Russell wear tight, 1930s-style evening gowns in bold leopard prints.

Dior called spring 1953's *Tulip* line 'the complete overthrowal of proportion, the expansion of the bust, and the effacement of the hips'. The wide top, he said, would make breathing easier. On the other hand, the constricted hips would make movement more difficult. Full skirts remained only for evening wear, otherwise skirts were tight and narrow, and worn with loose jackets.

Autumn 1953's *Living* line, Dior said, was inspired by the Eiffel Tower and the domes of Paris. Again, the Eiffel Tower-shape is a forerunner of the *A* line. Dior also abruptly raised hemlines to just below the knee, while his rival Balenciaga dropped them to the bottom of the calf. But in the battle of the hemlines, Dior, once again, won out.

Dior after the New Look

Dior's backer Boussac knew that the fuss over the New Look was a good thing. The Dior name was magic. In the 1940s, he was almost as well known as Stalin or Gandhi.

Rouët quickly used Dior's fame setting up a system of manufacturing garments under licence. Other couturiers followed suit and this system now brings them the bulk of their income.

In 1948, Dior went into the American ready-to-wear market. A new approach for couture, making two collections a year for them. Initially manufactured in New York, he found the work sloppy and had it transferred to Paris.

Dior's PR officer Harrison Elliot was an American, taken on as an English-speaking representative specifically to deal with the American market. For the autumn 1947 collection, Elliot packed the *SS America* out of New York with buyers. It was at his behest that Dior travelled to the US in September 1947 to collect his award from Neiman Marcus. America was conquered and eventually provided Maison Dior with 60 per cent of its sales.

Dior's three workrooms expanded to 28. His staff of 85 became 1,400. Twenty-five thousand customers passed through his salon each season, and distinguished guests dropped by to pay their respects.

Dior kept his work in the limelight by drawing inspiration from the style he had pioneered. He also worked on problems that confounded other designers. One was the slit in a tight skirt. Traditionally this opened to reveal the calf in a way that was vulgar to Dior, or on a fold that destroyed the line of the dress. Dior's skirts were

mounted on a taffeta sheath trimmed with a raised strip of the outer material, so the slit revealed what looked

like another skirt beneath. This doubled the time it took to make the skirt and doubled the price. But to those

who shopped at Dior, money was no object. Dior had made his house an institution. Dior was fashion.

Rouët established Dior Furs and at the other end of the market, stockings. Other couturiers looked down their

noses. Dior stockings, dresses brassieres, girdles, handbags, gloves, shoes, ties, swim-suits and jewellery

were made in eighty-seven countries, all paying royalties back to the ten companies set up under the Dior name.

The Petite Boutique in the Avenue Montaigne, which sold accessories, expanded to become the Grand Boutique

in Rue François 1er. Dior entered the perfume business with Miss Dior, a tribute to his sister. The English name

was designed to appeal to the American market. Two more companies were set up to distribute Dior perfume

and lipstick in France and America. He also set up branches in London, New York and Caracas. Companies in

Canada, Australia, Santiago and Cuba took reproduction contracts. But the heart of the firm was the house in

Avenue Montaigne. There, he had a clientele of three thousand women. Some of his creations were never

ordered. Most were copied forty times. Only the most successful were copied 150 times. Even

so, the output of his salon represented only a tiny percentage of the seven million dresses

sold every year in France.

THE NEW

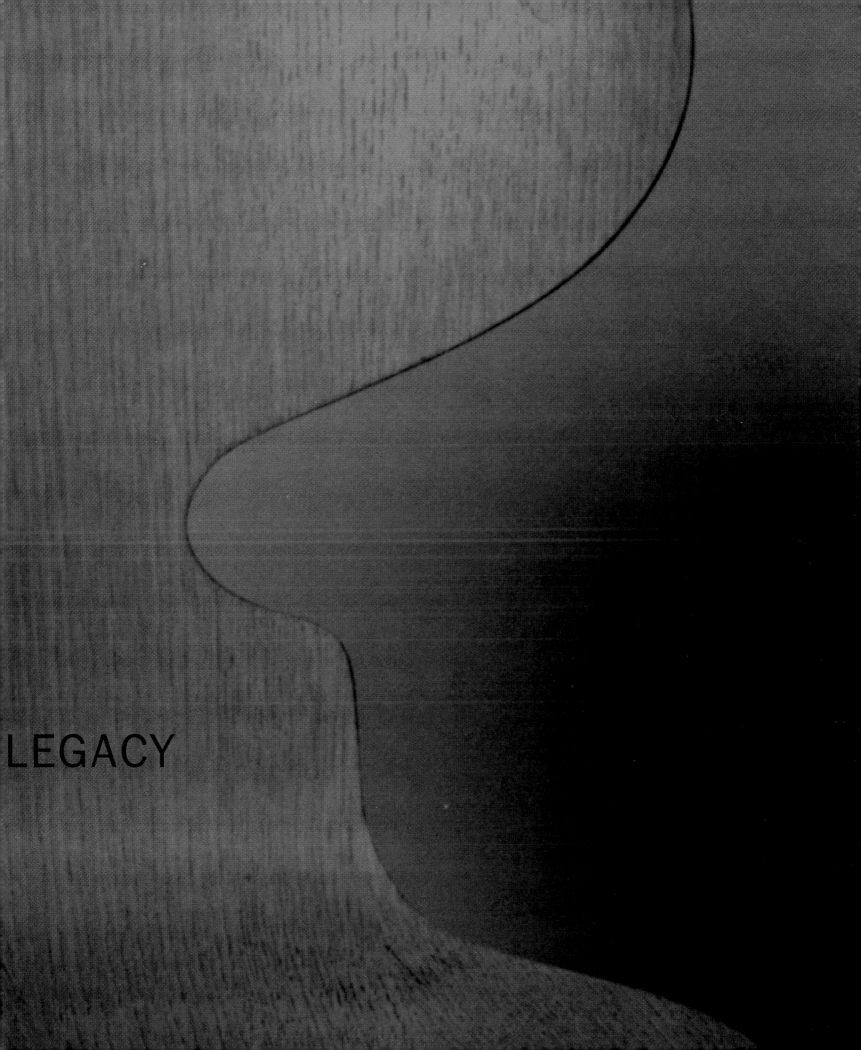

LEGACY

The long look of the *H*-line in a gently curving jacket
that typified the shoulderless, bustless and hipless
new looks of the 'French Bean' woman

This evening coat in satin from Dior's controversial 1954 collection was called 'grotesque' by some of the British press, adding that it looked 'suspiciously like a raincoat'

Above, Dior's model Renee with an outdoor ensemble in herringbone – one of the costumes that was shown at the Red Cross charity show at Blenheim Palace in November 1954

In 1954, Dior felt that he had exhausted all of the possibilities of the New Look. In spring, he reverted to the *Lily-of-the-Valley* line, but this was a short hiatus while he drew breath. Then he began a new revolution. He dumped seven years of the New Look. In a three-hour show that autumn, he amazed and outraged the fashion world with his new 'French Bean' woman. Also know as the *H* line or Flat look, the French Bean was shoulderless, hipless and bustless. The high rounded breasts, the slender waist and the curvaceous hips – direct, provincial ways of appealing to a man – were out. Marilyn Monroe – a woman who was built along New Look lines – said she felt insulted.

Instead, Dior had found a more subtle way of making women appealing. His dresses were fluid, loose fitting, adolescent. He introduced flowing blouses, sliding belts and revealed the legs – though never the knee which he regarded as the ugliest part of a woman's body. The bust disappeared, jackets fell straight to the hips and the parallel look of the 1920s was revived.

Seven years after reviving corseting with the New Look, it was going out of the window again. Many saw the influence of Molyneux here. He always stressed that garments should be wearable. Sadly, some of Dior's more radical New Look creations were definately not.

Once again the press attacked. The British papers were very critical, assailing Dior for reversing the trend that he himself had begun. But he took this in his stride. 'Better to be slated in three columns on the front page than congratulated in two lines on the inside,' he said.

A Dior white evening dress, picture by
Henry Clarke, that was featured in
Vogue in March 1954

Rivalry with Chanel Dior's New Look was one

of the reasons Coco Chanel came out of retirement. To her, Dior

was the epitome of a bad male designer. Instead of following the

fundamental shape of a woman's body, he imposed shapes on it.

He wanted to transform women to the shape of a flower, scissors,

a windmill, a letter A, H or Y, an oval or the Eiffel Tower. What's

more, his clothes were uncomfortable. A woman was meant to

stand around in the cold with her shoulders, arms and half her

bust exposed. The criticism was that Dior's women were meant to

be seductive ornaments for male consumption. To be fair, Dior

only designed for glamorous entertainers and the rich, who were

usually seductive ornaments to start with. And, after the austerity

of war, this is exactly what many women wanted to be.

The other couture houses were up in arms too. But there was nothing they could do about it. Dior was the king of *haute couture*. He was able to dictate fashion. The others had to follow suit and, though it is easy to see that a reaction to the New Look had already set in, no-one made such a great rejection of it as Dior.

Chanel, who re-emerged that year with a range of stylish suits, attacked him too.

'Balenciaga?' she said. 'He dresses women to look like old Spaniards. Dior? To look like armchairs. He put covers on them.'

Dior was amused rather than hurt. His only response was: 'Chanel had created a fashion for elegant women rather than those who are pretty.'

Although Dior acknowledged Chanel's place in the history of fashion, he thought she was not the master technician he was.

'Dresses must have a soul,' he said. 'In an age of machines, dressmaking has come to be the final refuge of all that his human, all that is personal, and all that can never be imitated.'

This sudden reversal was far too much for some customers, so in spring 1955, Dior backtracked with his *A* line. The lowered waistline of the *H* line was retained, but the fuller, more feminine forms of the Eiffel Tower returned. To subtly draw attention to this U-turn, all the names of the outfits: Alouette, Anglomania, Alliance – began with the letter A. There was even a waistless three-quarter-length coat worn over a short-sleeved vest dress with a pleated skirt called simply A.

One outfit, Adele, differed slightly from the original *A* line. It had a short-sleeve, shirt-waister top and was tightly clinched into a small waist in its natural position. The skirt was flared over net petticoats and reached just below the knee. This was to be the look every young girl adopted for the rest of the 1950s.

From narrow shoulders to a wide skirt, this outfit shows perfectly the *A*-line that Dior launched in 1955

Y

Sculptured satin

...sh tightly bound under
...bosom, one end thrown over
...oulder, the other falling down
...ront of the narrow skirt,
...es an Oriental character to Dior's
...onderful dress in pearl-grey satin

Described by *Vogue* as 'sculptured satin', the sash tightly bound
under a high bosom gave an Oriental character to Dior's *Y*-line
evening dress in pearl grey satin, Autumn 1955

A sketch by René Bouché from *Vogue* September 1957, illustrating the Dior *Spindle* line.
Far right, a Dior silk tube dress, inspired by the style of Indo-China

By winter 1955, Dior had turned the *A* line upside down and come up with the *Y* line. It was actually the *Tulip* line all over again, with the body forming a narrow stalk which opened out at the top. Dresses were narrow, shoulders wide.

However, the *A* and the *H* lines persisted, while the *Y* line had its waistline lifted to become the *Arrow* line in spring 1956.

Bulk remained at the top of the body in the *Magnet* line of autumn 1956. Huge scarves were used to add to this effect, while Dior dropped the hemlines back to the ankles. However, no-one else followed and, for the rest of the world, hemlines remained where Dior had put them in 1953.

The *Free* line of spring 1957 kept the Magnet's square-shouldered look – the very look Dior had overthrown ten years before. But it was clear the Dior was losing touch. One of his suits, Normandy, had a tubular jacket without sleeves. The wearer could not move her arms and it would have been impossible to put it on without the aid of a maid. Even for the richest woman, this was not exactly practical. And the chances of it being copied for ordinary women, who might need the use of their arms, was extremely slim.

Dior's last collection in autumn 1957 unveiled the *Spindle* line. Dresses were waistless sheaths, with curved side seams. Here, at last, he had come up with something comfortable to wear – how very different from the clothes that Dior had turned the world upside down with in 1947. It was a design imitated well into the 1960s.

The Successor – Yves Saint Laurent

In 1953, Michel de Brunhoff told Dior that he should take on the seventeen-year-old Yves Saint Laurent. Saint-Laurent had just won a fashion design competition organised by a textile manufacturer. Dior made Saint Laurent his assistant. He was even allowed to help Dior in the initial stages of design – something Dior had allowed no-one to help him with before.

In October 1957, Dior went to Rouët and told him that he felt Saint Laurent was not getting enough credit. By that time, Dior had worked closely with him for eighteen months and recognised his exceptional talent. Thirty outfits in Dior's final collection were based on Saint Laurent's designs and Dior thought the press should be told of his contribution.

But before anything could be arranged, at midnight on 24 October 1957, Dior complained of feeling unwell. Soon it was clear that nothing could be done. A priest was called and, soon after, Dior died. He was fifty-two.

Marcel Boussac naturally picked Yves Saint Laurent to replace Dior at Maison Dior. In his first collection, Saint Laurent took the *Spindle* line and the *Free* line and combined them with the *A* line to make his own *Trapeze* line. He was hailed by the press as the saviour of the Dior tradition. But then he started going his own way. By 1960, his Beat Look was drawing inspiration from bikers and students from the Left Bank. The chic women of Paris did not want to wear black leather suits, black woolly hats and black turtleneck sweaters. So Yves Saint Laurent, it was decided, had to go.

He was replaced by Marc Bohan who had worked at Piguet's, Molyneux's and Patou's before moving to Dior's London branch. He reverted to the waistless look of Dior's last two collections.

But times had changed. The youthful look had taken over and Paris fashion houses found it hard to compete with the English designers. Yves Saint Laurent had been right. He went on to set up his own fashion house.

Twenty-one year old Yves
Saint Laurent facing the
world's press after being
named the successor to
Christian Dior as chief
designer at the Dior salon,
in November 1957

The 'tulip' form instigated in fashion by Dior soon permeated much other design, like the famous Tulip glass, which was designed by Nils Landberg for Orrefors in 1947

Although after 1954, Dior had turned away from the New Look, the rest of the world had not. It had an impact on the whole of post-war design. Suddenly designers in every field felt they could make a break with the past and begin anew.

In Italy, there was a great explosion of energy and creativity called the *ricostruzione*. America's huge post-war boom in consumer goods led to many manufacturers encouraging new design to give them a competitive edge. And in Denmark, Sweden and Finland designers developed the Scandinavian Modern aesthetic. Many New Look concepts began turning up in ceramics, glass, silver, furniture, cars, radios, fridges and jukeboxes.

The New Look designers took their inspiration from the sculptural shapes Dior produced. These ideas fed though into all forms of three-dimensional design – even, ironically, architecture, where Dior had picked up many of these ideas in the first place.

The year of Dior's New Look, 1947, was the same year that Picasso took up ceramics. His fresh approach to this medium affected potters around the world and their output was immediately dubbed 'the New Look'. The German firm Rosenthal even called their new range of organic porcelain 'New Look' in 1955.

The application of the name 'New Look' outside the world of fashion is not without its justification. Just as Dior's New Look transformed the rigidly functional wartime clothing into sometime more aesthetically pleasing, the New Look in other forms of design attempted to transform the austere face of Modernism. Post-war designers, although still Modernists, wanted to make Modernism more visually and creatively satisfying and hence more appealing to a wider audience.

They inherited from pre-war Modernism a great commitment to purity of form and also clarity of outline. But the early Modern Movement thought that the shape of an object should be dictated by the object's function in a totally objective way, without adopting an arbitrary style. The post-war designers realised that this was not possible – Modernism was a style like any other.

The Tulip white moulded plastic chair by architect and designer Eero Saarinen, *very* **Fifties and** *very* **New Look**

Gio Ponti was also famous
for the long-legged chair
he innovated in 1957
called the *superleggera*

The New Look asserted that style element, seeing that elegance and exuberance were not necessarily an obstacle to good design. Those who took on this new aesthetic included Per Lütken in glass, Stig Lindberg in ceramics, Henning Koppel in silver, Charles Eames in furniture and Eero Saarinen in architecture. Saarinen's sculptural TWA Terminal at Kennedy Airport is pure New Look.

Many of Dior's New Look motifs turn up in other people's work. Dior wanted to make women look like flowers – especially tulips. Nils Landberg designed 'Tulip' glass vases for Orrefors. These were hand-blown to almost waferlike thinness with drawn-out bowls and needle thin stems. Landberg and Gunner Ander at Lindshammar also took the 'tulip' theme in their designs for glasses.

Eero Saarinen designed the 'Tulip' chair with a bud-shaped moulded white plastic seat and a single aluminium stem which splays out to a rounded pedestal. High-backed 'Tulip' chairs were being made in fibreglass right up to the end of the 1960s. The tulip shape was also to be found in light fittings of the period.

Dior's hourglass forms also proliferated. They turned up in Richard Latham and Raymond Loewy's 'Service 2000' a coffee service made for Rosenthal in 1954. Also in Waistel Cooper's waisted vases and Arne Jacobsen's Ant chair.

It has even been argued that, if it was not for Dior's hourglass forms, Marilyn Monroe might have remained a bit-part actress – instead of being the most famous hourglass figure of them all.

After the initial shock of the New Look, Dior started to stretch out the female figure – until he reached the *Long* line in 1951.

This elongation of form was taken up by Italian designers particularly. It can be seen in Gio Ponti's Pirelli Tower, those long-necked glass decanters he designed for Venini and the long thin legs of his famous *Superleggera* (Super Light) chairs. Alberto Giacometti took this elongated look even further in his sculpture. This is clearly evident in his *Femme Debout* in 1949, where the figure of a standing woman is drawn out to an almost sticklike thinness. Geofrey Bellamy's 1957 set of silver cutlery and Stuart Devlin's coffee set from 1959 too, both clearly employ this greatly exaggerated elongation. Dior's New Look re-introduced diagonal lines and asymmetry. His autumn 1948 show featured asymmetrical skirts and asymmetrical necklines. Other couturiers – particularly Dessès and Fath followed suit. So did many others including Finnish glassblowers, Danish silversmiths and Swedish ceramics makers.

In Denmark, Per Lütken experimented with ways to let glassware 'design itself' in asymmetrical and rounded 'New Look' forms. Venini produced 'Handkerchief' vases that ape the folds of Dior's cloth, while Paul Kedlves at Flygfors produced 'Coquille' bowls, where tear-drops of molten glass appear to have moulded themselves into a shell shape. Even Royal Dux in Czechoslovakia and Cmielow in Poland started producing extravagant asymmetrical tableware and ornaments.

The elongation of the female figure in the *Long* line became part of a design trend typified in the 1959 coffee set by British designer Stuart Devlin

The second wave of the New Look had to do with pattern and texture. In the very same year that Dior first produced his New Look, American artist Jackson Pollock created his first large-scale action paintings. These were hailed at the time 'a dynamic new aesthetic'. People had been starved of colour during the long dark years of the war. Now vivid primary colours exploded back on the scene.

Wallpapers and fabrics appeared with freer printed patterns which look like dye had been flung at them or flicked from a brush. Dior, himself, picked up on these. In 1953, he created his ready-to-wear suit from silk, with a blot design.

That same year Horrockses produced a fabric printed in black with an ink splash pattern. Aziz Martinelli produced a Pollock-style print in bold primary colours called Pirouette for Morton Sundour. And once the technique of photoprinting fabrics was perfected by the Swedish firm Stigens Fabriker in 1954 textile manufacturers began reproducing these wild splashed, squiggles and doodles produced by the action painters.

The 'New Look' of the action painters even spilled over into metalwork. Robert Welch came out with a seven-stick candelabrum, where the metal stems seemed to drip like a 3-D painting, after seeing and exhibition of Jackson Pollock's work in the Whitechapel Art Gallery in 1958.

Abstract expressionism found another home in glassware. Bright, bold coloured glass were swirled inside clear crystal. Max Verboeket in Maastricht manipulated these swirls into twisted, exaggerated forms. Norwegian glass maker Arne Jon Jutrem aped Pollock by dripping trails of molten coloured glass on to the surface of a ready-made vessel.

By 1963, the phrase New Look had become monstrously over used. There had been a New Look in furniture, a New Look in art, a New Look in jewellery, a New Look in daffodils and, in Britain, even a New Look Labour Party. In the English-speaking world, the term was gradually being replaced by 'contemporary'. But in Italy, Finland, Denmark and Sweden, the 'New Look' continued right up to the end of the 1960s.

The Dior 'hourglass' was most faithfully reflected in the memorable three-legged 'Ant' chair designed for Fritz Hansen in 1953 by the Danish architect-designer Arne Jabosen

Robert Welch's seven-stick candelabrum was inspired, like some of Dior's later fabric designs, by the 'drip' action paintings of abstract expressionists like Jackson Pollock

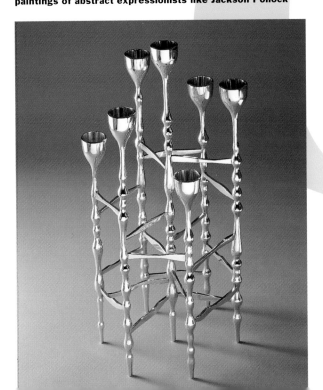

Dior always epitomised elegance; his Autumn collection
of 1953(right), Spring 1950 (the drawing by Eric) – all
reflected the classic New Look of 1947(opposite)

Dior after Dior

By 1970, Maison Dior realised it had to diversify or die. Marc Bohan designed a line of Christian Dior menswear.

This soon accounted for 40 per cent of their turnover and franchise shops were opened in Geneva, Madrid, Nice

and Cannes.

Meanwhile, the growth of man-made fibres left the Cotton King Marcel Boussac on the verge of bankruptcy. He

sold off Christian Dior Perfumes. But that did not save his textile empire. In 1978, the receivers were brought

it and Maison Dior was bought by Agache, who also financed Christian Lacroix. Nevertheless, the house that the

New Look built still stands today.

fin

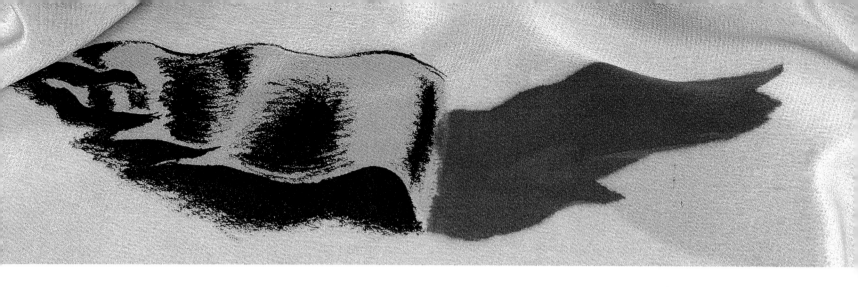

PICTURE ACKNOWLEDGEMENTS

Front and back cover, Hulton Getty Picture Collection **background**, Topham Picturepoint **main image.** Hulton Getty Picture Collection **front flap**, Topham Picturepoint **back flap.**

Advertising Archives **4 top, 24, 44 background, 46 bottom, 47 background, 51 background, 70.** Barnabys Picture library **49, 69 top, A Bruce 2/3.** British Film Institute Stills, **Posters and Designs 29 right.** Erwin Blumenfeld **"Doe Eye" January 1950. Used with kind permission of American Vogue. Photograph provided by Kathleen Blumenfeld 85, Lisa Fonssagrives sur la Tour Eiffel 1939. Dress by Lucien Lelong. Used with kind permission of French Vogue. Photograph supplied by Kathleen Blumenfeld 90.** Royal Pavilion, Art Gallery and Museums, Brighton **158/159, 173 top.** Camera Press **Cecil Beaton 152 centre.**

CASSINA S.P.A/Meda **699 "Superleggera" chair - Gio Ponti - 1/Aldo Ballo 170 bottom.** Courtesy of Sotheby's London **Cecil Beaton Photograph 87.** Center for Creative Photography **Copyright Louise Dahl-Wolfe Trust 146.** Jean-Loup Charmet **56/57, Berard Copyright DACS 1996 132, Drian Copyright ADAGP, Paris and DACS, London 1996 13, Gruau 150 top, Sam 110 top.** Corbis-Bettmann **11 top, 16, 52, 60, 69 bottom, UPI 8/9 top & bottom, 15, 28, 51, 56, 62, 83, 94, 128, 147 top, 148 top, 163, 165 centre.** Hamiltons Photographers Limited **Copyright Norman Parkinson Limited 1996 92, Horst P. Horst 32.** Robert Harding Picture Library **John G Ross 170 top.** Courtesy of Harpers Bazaar **120, 124, 140, by kind permission of Lillian Bassman 144, 145, by kind permission of Richard Dormer 93.**

Hulton Getty Picture Collection **6/7, 9 right, 11 background, 14/15, 17, 18, 19, 22, 31, 34, 36, 36/37 background, 39 centre, 40, 43 centre, 45 top, 45 bottom, 47 top, 48/49 background, 53, 58 top, 63, 64/65, 66/67 top & bottom, 67, 71 inset, 73 top, 73 bottom, 78 top, 95, 111, 121, 122, 123 right, 123 left, 125 top, 126 bottom, 126 right, 127 left, 147 bottom, 149 bottom, 156/57, 157, 167.** Kobal Collection **21, 25, 29 left, 74/75, 76, 76/77, 77, 80 top, 81 bottom, 20th Century Fox 81 top, Paramount 78/79 bottom, United Artists 79, Warner Bros 68 .** Copyright Man Ray Trust **ADAGP, Paris and DACS, London 1996 89.** Philadelphia Museum of Art **Gift of Elsa Schiaparelli. Jacket c. 1937. Schiaparelli, Elsa (French). Cocteau design copyright DACS 1996 26 top, Gift of Elsa Schiaperelli. Lobster Dress, c. 1937, Schiaparelli, Elsa (French) 26 bottom.** Popperfoto **42, 116, 117, 125 bottom.**

Courtesy of Sears, Roebuck and Co **72, Spring and Summer 1947 Catalog 100.** Topham Picturepoint **20/21, 30 right, 30 left, 58 bottom, 80 left, 96, 97 top, 98, 107, 109, 141, 142 top, 155 left, 156, 161 top, Associated Press 12 bottom, 41 top, 133, 150 bottom, 153 top, 155 right, Press Association 82, 161 centre.** Trans World Airlines, Inc **171.** By Courtesy of the Board of Trustees of the Victoria & Albert Museum **front endpapers, 43 background, 168, 169, 176, J. Stevenson 46 top.** Roger-Viollet **102 bottom, 118, Collection Viollet 57, Lapi-Viollet 41 bottom, 102.** Copyright British Vogue, Conde Nast Publications **54 top & bottom, 101 bottom, 101 top, 103 top, Balkin 110 bottom, 112 bottom right, 112 top left, 112 bottom left, 113 bottom left, 113 top right, 113 top right, 113 top left, 175, Cecil Beaton 48, 86, 97 bottom, Renee Bouche 165 top, Henry Clarke 137, 139,** **162, 164, Coffin back endpapers, 108, 134, 136, 138, 160, Denney 127 right, 142 bottom, 143, Andre Durst 33 bottom, Eric 12 top, 72, 174 right, Frances McLaughlin 154, Nepo 33 top, Nobile 140, Koren Radkai 4 bottom, Rawlings 39 top, 61, 152 top, 153 bottom, 174 top left, Rutledge 151.** Courtesy American Vogue **Copyright 1939 (renewed 1967) by the Conde Nast Publications Inc/Blumenfeld 35, Copyright 1942 (renewed 1970) by the Conde Nast Publications Inc. Vogue 55, Copyright 1942 (renewed 1970) by the Conde Nast Publications Inc/Rawlings 10/11 centre.** The Worshipful Company of Goldsmiths **172, 173 bottom.**